# MY LIFE IN SEARCH
# OF AFRICA

# MY LIFE IN SEARCH
# OF AFRICA

John Henrik Clarke

Third World Press          Chicago

07 06 05 04 03 02 01 00 99   5 4 3 2 1

Cover design by Angelo Williams

Library of Congress Cataloging-in-Publication Data
Clarke, John Henrik, 1915-
    My life in search of Africa/John Henrik Clarke.
        p.      cm.
    Originally published: Ithaca, N.Y.: Cornell University, Africana Studies and Research Center, 1994.
    Includes bibliographical references.
    ISBN 0-88378-158-1 (cloth:alk. paper)
    ISBN 0-88378-178-6 (pbk.: alk. paper)
    1. Clarke, John Henrik, 1915- . 2. Africanists—United States —Biography. I. Title.
DT19.7.C57A3 1999
973'.0496073—dc21
[b]                                                    97-48939
                                                          CIP

Third World Press
7822 S. Dobson
Chicago, IL 60619

To Drs. Bill and Camille Cosby
with appreciation for their help and
encouragement
which came at a time in my life when
it was most needed.

# CONTENTS

# INTRODUCTION

———•———

In a significant sense, John Henrik Clarke's entire life has been in search of Africa. His search is symbolic of the vision of Ethiopianists, Pan Africanists, and African centered thinkers throughout the European dominated modern world. Few, if any, have come closer than Dr. Clarke in recognizing the "Africa" which is within us all.

Professor Clarke's odyssey began when, as a small boy, his great-grandmother, Mary, told him stories about Africa and his brave African great-grandfather who fought against his enslavement. In his words, Dr. Clarke "began to search for people who looked like Africans" in the iconography of the bible culture which inundated the small Alabama and Georgia communities of his childhood. The absence of African images heightened his drive to find Africa. The absence also provided the foundation for his later rejection of a religion which had been given to us by our oppressors.

The three lectures which comprise this volume were delivered at Cornell University's Africana Studies and Research Center in March of 1990. The occasion was the celebration of the Center's twentieth anniversary. Indeed, Dr. Clarke was the role model for the establishment of the Center.

In these lectures, which were first published by Africana Studies and Research Center, John Henrik Clarke traces his intellectual development through Alabama, Georgia, Harlem, Africa, and the African World community. Most serious African thinkers throughout the world either know or are familiar with the quest of Professor Clarke. He has been involved in the significant moments of the Pan African Project since the 1930s when he reached Harlem.

In the first lecture, Dr. Clarke sketches his journey from the inquisitive black boy in search of the Africa his great-grandmother told stories about, through his apprenticeship with the master teachers in Harlem such as Arthur Shomberg, J. A. Rogers, and Willis N. Huggins. It was during this latter period that he formed a lifelong intellectual friendship with John G. Jackson. These Pan African scholars researched, studied, and taught together in the Harlem History Club and later the Blyden Society, named for one of the fathers of Pan Africanism, Edward Wilmot Blyden. Blyden had pioneered African unity in the Caribbean, North American, England, and the African continent.

John Clarke's master teachers were also involved in the struggle for Africana freedom and independence. "Huggins went to Geneva to see what was happening in relationship to the war in Ethiopia." J. A. Rogers went to the battlefront in Ethiopia and reported back to the members. Thus, the scholars fought for the liberation of African peoples in the intellectual, political, and military arenas. Ethiopia was important because it was the only African country which had maintained its freedom after the European colonization which followed the Berlin Conference. It was a metaphor for the historical unity and significance of African peoples.

Dr. Clarke's narrative, while focused on the project, revealed the struggles of a dedicated African man as he eked out a living while pursuing a career as a writer, lecturer, and social activist. His African dignity radiated as he went from job to job, elevating the status of work which is often thought of as menial. Little "Fess," as he was called in high school, took his great spirit through World War II where he was a master sergeant who protected the soldiers under his command. Looking back at this experience, Dr. Clarke said, "After leaving the army disenchanted, I tried to pick up my career as an Africanist again."

Subsequent to his return from service, Professor Clarke was involved as an "independent socialist" and sometimes "fellow traveler of the Communist Party." He emphasized, however, "I am a Nationalist and a Pan Africanist, first and foremost." Therefore, his association with socialism and communism was always subordinate to his life in search of Africa.

In 1958, Dr. Clarke had "saved up enough money to go to Africa." In Ghana, he met J. B. Danquah and met again with Kwame Nkhrumah whom he had met earlier in Harlem, when Nkhrumah was in the U.S. He also visited Togo and Nigeria, and was adopted by the Ewe who claimed he was a son who had returned. On the return trip, he met Alioune Diop, the great Senegalese publisher of *Presence Africaine*, which in turn led to his meeting with Cheikh Anta Diop.

By this time the Civil Rights Movement was in full swing, and John Clarke was fully prepared to provide guidance to the black students who took the leadership of the movement in the decade of the sixties. When the students began to demand Black Studies, Professor Clarke was ready—ready to provide a curriculum which their demands required.

The second lecture deals with Dr. Clarke's role as builder of the discipline of Africana Studies. When the African scholars and students seceded from the African Studies Association in 1969 and formed the African Heritage Studies Association, Dr. Clarke was in the forefront. He played a major role in establish-

ing the Africana Studies program at Cornell
University. At the same time, he played a similar part
in the instituting of the Black and Puerto Rican
Studies Department at Hunter College.

He speaks lovingly of his students whom he
inspired to reject the easy path to "education," and
take the higher ground of educational excellence, in
pursuit of the attainment of true liberation. It was
during this period that he formed his friendship and
collegial argumentation with Yosef ben Jochannan.
They spurred each other to greater and higher levels
of instruction. A revival of Pan African discourse followed their trajectory.

Not only did Professor Clarke play a major part
in establishing the discipline and inspiring students
in general, in the meantime he encouraged young
scholars to begin research writing and publication.
In this vein, he convinced a publisher to translate
and publish several of Diop's works.

In the final lecture, Dr. Clarke turns to the
problem of historiography and the future agenda of
Pan African scholarship. He explains the colonization of our history and the exclusion of African historians from world history, asserting that he is not a
"revisionist" but a "correctionist."

In Professor Clarke's opinion, Africans can
best change the world by changing ourselves first. To
promote that kind of change, John Henrik Clarke has
become a role model for African Eldership; those of
us who are his disciples are struggling to hold erect
the staff that he has passed to us.

Let us close this preface with John's profound
and eloquent speech, as he summarized his search at
the end of the second lecture:

"In my search for African history, I have had
a second beginning because this pursuit

has been for me a priesthood. . . I have established a community of students and scholarly colleagues and friends."

He continued as he thought about himself:

A sharecropper's son from the backwoods of Alabama, growing up in a family that did not read any book except the Bible. Growing up poor and hungry; mowing lawns, washing dishes, shining shoes, airing dogs, coming to New York and working in hotels, all kinds of night jobs and day jobs, studying at night and working in the day, and sometimes studying in the day and working at night. I was in pursuit of the definition of the role my own people had played in the history of the world; this had been my holy mission, my priesthood. I hope it can be said, whenever the end comes, and 1 am not hurrying it, because I have no objection to living a thousand years, and I would be useful every day of that time. However, when it is all over, and when I have made every contribution I can make, I hope it can be honestly said of me, "He did the best he could with what he had."

John Henrik Clarke has done much more than the whole company of the rest of us. He has been an exemplary model of the African who possesses the Good Speech and profound wisdom which is essential for the intergenerational transmission of knowledge which is the life blood of African life!

Jacob H. Carruthers

# PART I

EARLY AWARENESS

# EARLY AWARENESS

As I look back over the last twenty years, and take a brief inventory of the results of having taught more than a generation of students, I can name among my former students at least eleven who are heads of Black Studies programs, two former ambassadors, three cultural attaches, about seven medical doctors, and two who have risen to high positions in White law firms. This alone makes my career as a teacher worthwhile. And if I have a hereafter, this might be my hereafter.

I want to begin at the beginning because to a great extent I am a contradiction. I had to work against all of the odds to succeed, but succeed I did, although by the measurement of White sociologists, I was not supposed to make it at all. I was born into a family that was extremely poor, that was separated by the search for work a great deal of the time, where the only book in the house was the Bible, and where the beginning of my reading awareness was around the church and the Sunday School. Yet, my awareness of Africa, and my search for its definition in history began very early in my life, sitting at the feet of my great-grandmother, who kept telling me African stories. She had the turkey concession in our family. If you know the formation of farm families, someone would have the tobacco concession and would be responsible for the tobacco patch. My great-grandmother was responsible for the turkeys, and I was always helping her with those turkeys, running up and down the hill while she's telling me African stories. I did not know the significance of those stories

until much later. The one story she kept telling me
repeatedly was the story of her first husband who
was sold to a slave breeding farm in Virginia.

After emancipation, she went into Virginia and
spent three years looking for him. She said he was
brave like in Africa. She kept emphasizing his African
bravery. He stood up, he fought back. He was a
man. She emphasized how tall he was. Sometimes,
I would see three generations of my family in one
room all at the same time—my father and his generation, my grandfather and his generation, my grand
aunt Liza, the midwife. My great-grandmother would
tell her story anywhere three or more were gathered,
then she would turn to my grandfather, her son, who
was my father's father, and say, "Jonah, that was
your father." She would remind him of this African
named "Buck" who was sold to a slave breeding farm
in Virginia. He was so brave and so strong they sold
him so he could breed other African slaves to be
brave and strong. Or at least to be strong, because
no one breeds a slave to be brave.

She would tell me the stories because I would
listen. I was a favorite of hers and when I did something wrong, she made sure that she did the punishing. When she said, "Send the boy to me," I felt
happy and safe. At a hundred and eight, how hard
can she hit? "Bring me a switch, boy," and I brought
her the switch or a strap. Her hitting was like hugging. Then she would hit me and her arm would
almost go around me as though she was hugging and
apologizing at the same time, but the hitting didn't
hurt very much anyway. Then, I would go through
this fake crying; and when it was all over, I would sit
there, and she would tell me African stories, and
great adventures that she had gone through.

She said she was a slave in Georgia when
Sherman was marching to the sea. "Meanest man I

ever saw, "she said, "eyes redder dan a coon." One of
the adults would say, "Ma Mary, you know you didn't
see his eyes." "I'se seed it! I'se seed it!" When we'd
dispute her some more, she would stand up and tap
her cane on the floor; that meant the Supreme Court
had met and rendered its decision. There was no
reprieve. No more arguments. She saw Sherman
march to the sea, and his eyes were redder than a
coon, and she did "seed it," not see it; she "seed it."
And that was the end of that.

She said she witnessed the last Africans
brought over directly from Africa, who had not as yet
learned English, and they spoke in grunts. She was
my connection. She was the first person to bring to
my attention the strength of Africans, and to plant
the word Africa in my mind.

A disaster happened, and my father moved the
family to Columbus, Georgia. I wanted to teach the
junior class in Sunday School, so I learned to read
very early. Great-grandmother Mary was a Baptist
cultist. She thought that anybody who wasn't a
Baptist was somewhat off in their religious direction
anyway. She would wish them well, and as they left
the house she would extend her hand and say: "Run
the race of life, and run it by faith." Then, by the time
they got down the road she would start preaching a
sermon about Methodists who get sprinkled and
"God said nothing about being sprinkled. He said:
'Be immersed in the water. Be baptized.' Why can't
they understand it?" Methodists she could not understand at all, and she had lots of pity for the poor
sprinkled people. Yet, she had a quiet love even for
them.

My point here is that I wanted to teach Sunday
School, and she had taught me that God was love,
and God was merciful, and God was the father of all
people whom he loved equally. She had also taught

me about Africa. When I opened the Bible, I saw no
one who looked like an African—I could find no image
of my people in God's book. I encountered my first
contradiction. I began to search for people who
looked like Africans. I saw Moses, who was born in
Goshen, which was in Egypt and is still in Egypt.
Moses gets White. Moses goes down to Ethiopia and
marries Zippora; Zippora gets White. People go into
the land of Kush, the present-day Sudan; they get
White. People go to Punt, which is present-day
Somalia, and they get White. They were all depicted
as White in the illustrations in my Bible that deals
with African people. The fact that I could not find
Black people in Africa made the contradiction com-
pound itself in my mind. I was confused; I was
taught that God is love, and it was beginning to look
as if God who loved all people had left an entire people out of "his Book." I was told the book is his holy
word, yet I was learning in the same book that God
cursed Ham for looking at his father's nakedness. I
could not accept as fact that God could love and
curse his people at the same time. I could not believe
that God could discriminate against his own children. This led me into a religious contradiction that
was to take me twenty years to work out.

　　Twenty years would pass before I would read
Sir James Fraser's *Folklore Of The Old Testament*.
Twenty years would pass before I would discover that
the Bible is mainly Jewish folklore. That it is really a
Jewish survival book, and a good one. That these
stories were told to illustrate truth and morality, and
that if you tell a story to illustrate truth and morality, if the truth gets across, the illustration you used
to make the point need not necessarily be the truth.
This is a point that most Black people do not understand even to this day. There were allegorical stories
that were told in an age when people did not read

books.  People would tell stories to illustrate a point.

Now, let me tell you a simple African story Chinua Achebe told at New York University a few months ago, before he went to Africa, met with an accident, and is now seriously ill in London:

> A frog was walking down the street, or down
> a road.  A snake passed on a horse; he was
> riding the horse.  The frog frowned at the
> snake and said: "Oh my God, Mr. Snake,
> you don't know how to ride a horse.  You're
> a terrible rider." So the snake got down, and
> let the frog show him how to ride the horse.
> Finally, the snake conceded that the frog
> could indeed ride a horse better than he.  As
> he galloped away he said to the frog: "To
> know is one thing.  To have is another." The
> frog was still walking, but the snake had a
> horse, and he was riding—this was the
> point.

Don't let my saying that animals could talk bother you.  Concentrate on what I said the animals said.  The African in his infinite wisdom could have believed that if God made the oceans he had to turn the seasons; turn the leaves green on one side of the world, turn them brown on the other side of the world, make the oceans roll on one side of the world, make rain on another side of the world, and make a hurricane on another side of the world.  God was so busy that he didn't have time to give the animals the gift of talk.  So, the Africans decided to do that for Him.  This is the origin of African animal talking stories.  They thought they were doing God's work.  Now, if you understand African animal-talking stories, and you look at Malcolm X's stories—illustrating his points through stories, the fox and snakes, and the grass—all Malcolm was doing was illustrating something with animal-talking stories.

My point is this. As a Sunday School teacher, I was to learn that the Sunday school lessons came from a White Baptist printing company in Nashville, Tennessee. If the writers were White, and the staff of the Baptist printing company were White, then the image they portray would normally be White.

Twenty years would pass before I would understand that when the Europeans emerged in the world in the fifteenth and sixteenth centuries, for the second time, they not only colonized most of the world, they colonized information about the world. They also colonized images, including the image of God, thereby putting us into a trap, for we are the only people who worship a God whose image we did not choose. That was our trap then, it is our trap now. We cannot conceive of a God that looks like us. This is why right now we will fight each other quicker than we would fight anything with a White face. We could rationalize plunging a knife into one of us, but we cannot rationalize plunging a knife into a White policeman who is mutilating a Black woman or a Black man. We are trapped by this White image, and a lot of these images came straight out of the Bible.

My contradictions then, the contradictions I would have to work out, were all these White angels. If God is love, with all the brown people in the world, with all the Black people in the world, all the yellow people in the world, shouldn't one little yellow, brown or Black angel sneak into heaven some way or somewhere? One that has been good enough to get into heaven. What is this saying to you? That a people who control the power of the world and control the images of the world, are saying to you, that heaven is even reserved for them and their kith and kin. Not only do they reserve earth for themselves, they reserve heaven for themselves.

It took this wonderment of my findings about the Bible to stir memories of my early school years. I longed for an education, and finally, I would go to a city school. Only one child in a family who lived outside of the city limits was allowed to go to school in the city, and I was chosen from among my nine brothers and sisters to go to a city school. I went to the Fifth Avenue school in Columbus, Georgia, from the third grade through the sixth. When I was in third grade, I was assigned to write a composition. I was working before and after school running errands for army officers; I was so sleepy I went to bed without having my composition ready in the morning. I got up with a blank piece of paper, and read a complete fabrication in class. I made the whole thing up. The teacher said, "John . . ." she's still alive incidentally, she's about ninety-two, ". . . hand that in. This is a good example of fine writing." I didn't have anything on the paper, and she decided, instead of punishing me, she would encourage me to pursue a career as a writer. I never thought about writing until then, but then I began to seriously think about it.

When I began to write, I wasn't writing stories, I was writing songs. Mostly songs about local things. Fourth grade was not too adventurous, but in my fifth grade I met a great teacher. Also, I ran into something—rather, I noticed it—that was there all along, but we don't talk about it much in these days. Most of the dark-skinned kids went to Miss Taylor and Miss Dent, and the light-skinned kids went to Miss Fontrice and another teacher. Being dark enough to go to Miss Taylor was the greatest thing that could have ever happened to me. Miss Taylor was one of the greatest teachers ever. I was late in arriving in the fifth grade because I had to take time away from school to help my father who was a part-time farmer. I was about 14 when I entered the fifth grade. I had left home, and was self-sustaining. I began playing the fool in class because I wanted to be accepted by the students. I mean I was bowing to peer pressure. Miss Taylor called me into her room during her lunch hour, and closed the door. I noticed that Miss Dent wasn't there; they generally had their lunch together, but she was out. It was just the two of us now and she read me the riot act. "Your days of playing the fool are over. I'm going to tell you what education is, and what it's supposed to do for you. Stop worrying about being alone. You want to be accepted. If people cannot accept you the way you are, then do without them. You're not going to die from walking alone. If you are right, you will not really be alone." Then she told me what education was, what she expected of me, and she said, "I will never let you be less than your best self." Then she raised my face held it between her hands and looked me dead in the eye—I couldn't look to the right or to the left—and said something that every child needs to be told at least once in his or her life-time, simply: "I believe in you. I have confidence in you. I believe you'll make it."

I've had three deities in my life, all women. My great grandmother, my mother, who died when I was seven, and Miss Evelina Taylor. Every time I tried to get into mischief, I'd imagine one of those women looking over my shoulder, saying "Uh uh," while tapping me on the arm. "That's not nice. John, you know you shouldn't do that." They've kept me out of temptation. I'm glad they did because they made me a better human being. They set a standard for me and made me set a standard of integrity for myself, and my human relationships, with both men and women. It was in Miss Taylor's room that I decided to do something exceptional. On Fridays we had current events, and I wanted to lecture on African people in ancient history.

I went to a White man (if he is alive today he is a liberal capitalist), named Gagsteider, a lawyer, who had a good library. I had been taking the books from the library. He hadn't missed them so I stopped bringing them back. I asked for a book on ancient history, and as we say in the South he let me down slow. He said very kindly, "John, I'm sorry, but you came from a race of people who have no history. If you persevere, keep clean and work hard, and obey, you might make history one day." Then he prophesied for me the greatest thing a White man could prophesy for a Black man in the days when I was growing up, "One day you might be a great Negro like Booker T. Washington." I didn't know anything about Booker T. Washington then, and twenty years would pass before I could check him out. I didn't even know it was supposed to be a compliment until later on. My mind rebelled against the concept that I came from a people who had no history.

Finally, I was working; shining shoes, working for officers, airing dogs, washing dogs, doing anything to survive. Disagreement with an evil stepmother led me to leave home. I was living in a boarding house, which became another kind of house that you don't discuss in the presence of ladies. Miss Rosalie was kind to me, and the ladies of the house were as kind to me, as much of a family to me as any other family I ever had. They bought me books and gave me money to put into the church collection, a little money for some clothing I needed, and they put money together and bought me a set of Winston Encyclopedias—for $36.00! That's a whole lot of money considering that their trade wasn't paying very much during that period. That's how I remember them, with great affection. Now, I was the only one that had a set of encyclopedias in the neighborhood, so other students came to me to get help with their homework.

When I was ten, even before I had the encyclopedias, I was called "Little Fess," or "Little Professor." This is why the word doctor doesn't stir any romance inside of me, but the word professor gives me a feeling over and above doctor, because this is what I seem to have been for a long time, "Little Professor." I had a phenomenal memory and because of this, and because I wanted to do something exceptional for Miss Taylor, I was looking for something on ancient history. I could find little. Later on, doing chores at the local high school, I came upon an important book. (I wasn't in high school formally—grade wise, I did not reach high school. The seventh grade was so big and the high school was so new and uncrowded, they put the seventh grade in the high school building. So I was able to enjoy the high school and it's atmosphere.)

While there, I began to do chores because the "Black Brigade" did the chores. The "Black Brigade" were the dark-skinned children, as against the "Light Brigade" who were the light-skinned children and who received favorable treatment in the schools. These children appeared in the school plays and were usually middle-class children who wore shoes all year round and ate three meals a day, every day. They were freaks to us, you know, odd balls. While doing chores I met this man who was trying to raise some money for the curtain for the high school's stage. His name was Jones. He had a book called *The New Negro*. While I was holding his coat, I was holding his book. I opened it to an essay entitled "The Negro Digs Up His Past" by Arthur Schomburg, a Puerto Rican of African descent. For the first time I knew that we not only had an ancient history, but we are an old people; that we were already old before Europe was born; that half of human history was over before we knew Europeans were in the world; and that we had built great civilizations that not only had no jail system, but had no word in their language that meant jail. I was not only beginning to develop some security, I was beginning to look at White people with smugness; I thought, "Young things, you just got here ...we've been here a long time." Then I began to understand that slavery was something that touched the lives of all people on earth, and that the period of our enslavement was short in comparison to the period when Europeans enslaved Europeans.

At the height of Greek Civilization, 85% of the Greeks were slaves to other Greeks. With all their talk about democracy, most of the Greeks were slaves. All the time the Romans were talking about democracy in the senate, many of the Romans were slaves. The feudal period in Europe was the period of European enslavement of Europeans. I began to seriously study slavery as an entity in human history, and finally I would go to the 135th Street library. I knew Arthur Schomburg was there. I thought he was an intellectual in a great tower with people guarding him, to keep people from stealing his knowledge. I humbly asked the clerk at the counter downstairs: "Do you know anybody that could give me a letter to see Arthur Schomburg?" She was short tempered and she said, "You'll just have to walk up three flights!" I said, "Good God!" So I walked up three flights; the Schomburg collection was on the top floor then. I stood in the door and saw this imposing man. Arthur Schomburg was a handsome man, but very imposing. He was sitting at the desk, guarding it while the rest of his staff was out to lunch. He said, "Come in, son. Sit down," and I did.

I told him I wanted to know all the history of

the Negroes, all the history of Africa henceforth, right
now, within the hour—his lunch hour. He said, "Son,
what you're calling Negro history and African history
are the missing pages of world history." He said:
"Son, go study the history of your masters. Go study
the history of Europe. If you understand the history
of Europe, you will understand how you got left out
of history, who left you out, and why you got left out
of history. You will understand something else; no
oppressor can successfully oppress a consciously
historical people because a consciously historical
people would not let it happen. It became a necessi-
ty to remove you from history in order to convince
you, at least in part, that you are supposed to be
oppressed; to remove from your eyesight every image
of endearment, everything that endears you to yourself, so you can feel that, at least in part, God, too has
frowned on you, and deserted you, and put you outside the basis of humanity."

I began to read European history. I began to
read *An Old Chestnut*, which is still worth reading if
you want a good general outline of European histo-
ry/world history. At that time you could buy it from
a drugstore for fifty-nine cents. I also read H.G.
Wells's *Outline of History*. Soon I began to go to the
library and check out six books and take them back
and check out six more. I began reading all kinds of
books on history, and when I came back to African
history I saw it clearly. At the same time I was participating in the National League of Negro Youth. I
joined the Harlem History Club under Dr. Willis N.
Huggins. There, while under Willis Huggins, I began
to learn the political meaning of history. While
studying under Schomburg, I learned the interrela-
tionship of African history to world history. Later on,
by listening to the lectures of William Leo Hansberry
of Howard University, I learned the philosophical

meaning of African history. Now you've got these great masters such as Raphael Powell, alive and preaching in Harlem. He'd written a book called *The Human Side of A People And Their Right Name*, debunking the word Negro, calling attention to the fact that the proper name of any people must always relate to land, history and culture. I was to meet Charles Seiford, who had written a book, *The African Origins Of The Concept Of The Brotherhood Of Man*, which is still unpublished. He'd written another book, also unpublished, entitled *Who Are The Ethiopians?* This is a book of letters written to different White historians, arguing over the place of Ethiopia in world history. He had one hang-up. A lot of people thought he devoted too much time to it. He believed that the ancient Jews and the Africans were one and the same. They could have been, but I just don't think it's an argument worth a great deal of my time. If they were, so they were. There were some people of the Hebrew faith from western Asia who came into Africa and stayed for a period of over 200 years. The reason for their coming and the reason for their leaving Africa is still a subject of debate. In the Harlem History Club, Dr. Willis N. Huggins introduced me to certain aspects of the South African labor movement, especially the career of Clements Kadalie of Nyasaland. He introduced me to John Tengo Jabau, a forerunner of Nelson Mandela, Oliver Tambo and John L. Dube.

John L. Dube went to a college in South Witwatersrand, which is still in existence. Being the first Black to go to this Boer university which was run by the English, he had to go to school in a top hat and a frock coat in all that African heat, dressed up like he was going to a wedding. He was so accepted by Whites, until he wrote a scurrilous book called *The Black Man Is His Own Worst Enemy*. When he final-

ly understood what a fool he was, he took off all that
garbage, and went from village to village building the
African National Congress (A.N.C). The A.N.C. is a
worthy organization when you think of how it was
built and the people who sacrificed to build it; so is
the NAACP. Yet one has gone as wrong as the other—
one today is as misguided and as off cue as the other.
I'm talking about the people who built the original,
which took a lot of sincere work—a lot of radical
work.   When you think that both of these organizations are basically conservative now—you will see
that many things that are conservative now were radical in their original form.   From Clements Kadalie, I
would learn the basic history of trade union movements in South Africa.   I read some of the letters
between A. Philip Randolph and Clements Kadalie.   I
read the old *Messenger.* I read an essay by Clements
Kadalle still worth reading, "The Growth of South
African Trade Unionism."

An Ugandan teacher who was married to a
Black American came among us, Ernest Kalabala.
We learned about another aspect of Africa from him.
We supported missionary schools, where the children
paid thirty dollars a year in tuition.   We adopted one
child and became responsible for that child's school
fees, while we were working and making $15 to $16 a
week.   Finally, I worked up to become the second
salad man in a cafeteria.   I then made $18.50 a week,
and wore a tweed overcoat imported directly from
England, on which I paid $2.00 a week and finally got
it paid off.   There was my shined shoe period; when I
got dressed, I didn't wear anything that I hadn't
shined.   My suede period—the dandiest little radical
in all of Harlem.   I almost got expelled from the radical group because I looked too bourgeois.   I was
learning about doing a whole lot of other things.   I
met John G. Jackson; he and Willis Huggins had put

together two books, *A Guide to the Study of African History* and *An Introduction to African Civilization.* John Jackson rewrote that book under another but basically the same title. When I arrived in New York in 1933, and entered the club in 1934, John G. Jackson had already written his little book, *The African Origins of the Legend Of the Garden of Eden,* and another one; *Was Jesus Christ A Negro?* He later wrote *Pagan Origins of the Christ Myth,* tracing the Christ story through twenty-six civilizations, all a thousand miles apart, showing that all different people have their Christ story and that all different people have their creation stories. You know one story and you swear by it, but Africa has some of the most beautiful creation stories in the world, though all you know about is Adam and Eve and Noah.

There are South Sea Island creation stories and South Sea Island flood stories. If you read Sir James Fraser's *Folklore Of The Old Testament,* one of the parts he devoted most space to was the deluge or flood stories. When you look at the world from a point of view willed to you by your oppressor, you quite forget that there's a whole lot of people with different concepts of God in different places in this world. So therefore, I began to read religious literature. I did not lose the concept of God, but I gained the concept of spirituality which is higher than the concept of religion. I'm not going to fight you on this, I'm just explaining to you that spirituality was here before religion was here and that foreigners turned spirituality into religion and turned the religions against each other, and said that God ordained what they were doing, therefore making God a bigot, and an accomplice to their deeds. You have not examined religion well enough to understand that you can be a very highly spiritual person on this earth without buying any of it. I dare you to walk this earth without some form of spirituality. For atheists, no God becomes their God. No God becomes their Godliness. I maintain that humans cannot live without spirituality. Our real spirituality becomes our rebellion and our seeking. We cannot exist without some spiritual guidance. That is what separates humans from animals.

Then came the period of the Italian-Ethiopian war, beginning in 1935. Willis Huggins decided to go to Geneva; we raised most of the money with our small salaries. Huggins went to Geneva to see what was happening in relationship to the war in Ethiopia. Part of the money was raised by us for J.A. Rogers to go to the battlefront and report back to us. We had this kind of alertness then. While Huggins was away, not being able to give his regular Sunday morning lectures, the young Turks took over. John Jackson delivered the first lecture, "The Black Man As An Imperialist: When Blacks Ruled Whites," dealing with Africans in Spain and in the Mediterranean, and dealing with the world when Egypt ruled western Asia. We didn't have tape recorders then, and a lot of times people did not take notes.

I delivered the second lecture, "An Inquiry Into The Racial Identity Of Jesus Christ." I was twenty-two or three, and when you're that age you think you know everything; however, at that age you don't know anything for sure. Out of that lecture and from what I had learned in the old Harlem History Club, I was beginning to write short stories and they began to appear in *Opportunity* magazine. I set up a conspiracy between myself and a man named Edward Lawson, then the managing editor. I would have one of my stories in one issue, and he would have one of his articles in the next. The first story of mine that appeared was called "On The Other Side," dealing with a mulatto passing for White in England. The story tells of a Black gospel group who was giving a performance in England. In the audience was a mulatto who was passing for White. He allowed the music and his blackness to get the best of him, and almost jumped up and shouted and gave away his secret. However, he was able to control himself. When he calmed down, he realized what a fraud he was by denying his birthright.

The second story to appear was on the honor roll of the Best Short Stories of the Year. It was called "Santa Clause is a White Man." Of the two stories written about growing up in Columbus, Georgia, this one was the best. I was curious to know if anybody in Columbus, Georgia knew that their little star had gone North and made something out of himself. I used a fictitious situation; I used the name of living people and based it on an incident in Miss Taylor's fifth grade classroom. It was about a kid who painted a picture of Christ for his teacher that resembled his father, and a principal who defended the boy's right to paint God to resemble his father because the deity in all cultures is depicted to resemble the fathers in the culture. The principal subsequently lost his job for defending the boy. The story was called "The Boy Who Painted Christ Black."

It was a gimmick story. I wrote it in about 45 minutes—during that time I would draft a story about three times before I would start writing a final version. I was a very careful writer. This I wrote in one sitting. I went to the 124th Street library to call on a young lady who was working on a WPA (Works Progress Administration) Youth project in the library. At that time, I was preaching the gospel according to Karl Marx, and I was calling anybody a dirty capitalist at the slightest opportunity. The girl told me she would have to work an hour longer. I was beginning to say her boss was a "dirty, exploiting capitalist.

Why do they do this to you? We have to change this system." So she came over and brought me some paper and said: "Why don't you write dear, do something useful?" She came back and whispered, "John, I need the job." So, I wrote that story—it had been hanging in my mind anyway. When it was finished, I picked up the paper and we went wherever we were going, usually to some demonstration. My career as a writer was underway.

Into the Harlem History Club, after Huggins returned, came a young student, Francis K. Nkrumah. That was his name at that time. He was always broke, and his entertainment was walking down the streets of Lenox Avenue and Seventh Avenue arguing with the street speakers who spoke from step ladders, with a girlfriend on his arm. There used to be parlors where you could buy imitation ice cream called icies; he didn't even have ten cents to buy her an icie. One of his girlfriends was a nurse at Harlem Hospital; she's still living. She had to quit this African because he didn't even have the price of a movie, which was 20 cents at that time. He was studying to be a minister, and we would argue with him. We'd say, "Man, Africa don't need no ministers. Ethiopia just got her tail beaten. What Africa needs is soldiers, Africa needs to hit somebody. At least a carpenter, something." We would argue with him, and he would never answer until he got his answer ready. When he got it together, he was devastating. He was a great practical joker. Very few people got to know him personally. After he won the argument (and he knew he would always win) he would point his finger at you and tap you on the back and say, "Uh-huh, I got you, I got you." He was a joyful human being, a very nice human being. He had a beautiful laugh and his teeth were so white they looked artificial. Nnamdi Azikiwe, whom we called

Zeke, was teaching in America then and he would come by. It was the home of a lot of Africans.

During this time, the African Academy of Arts and Letters came into being, with A. A Nwafro Orizu, K. Ozuomba Mbadiwe, and the great Nigerian crowd; students from the Gold Coast, later called Ghana, also came by. We were together then. African students lived in Harlem. This was before independence, before the downtown people were accepting them, and before they were chasing after every White girl in sight. If they had a girl at that time, she was Black. They were content to eat in the neighborhood, the same greasy-spoon restaurants we all ate in. All of this was leading to the conflict of the Second World War.

Nkrumah disappeared, leaving for England with a letter of introduction from C.L.R. James to George Padmore, suggesting that Padmore straighten out Nkrumah's thinking. He said that Nkrumah might amount to something one day. He is a fair African nationalist who seems to be a little politically confused. Nkrumah took the letter, he didn't open it. Years later when I was in Ghana, he invited C.L.R. James to a big banquet, opened the letter, read it and laughed so much he fell off his seat. "Do you think I'll amount to anything now that I'm head of a state?" This is the kind of practical joker he was.

When he saw me in Africa, he was coming home from a state matter and everybody was lined up on the sidewalk hailing the president. He saw me, the car stopped and the guards jumped out, thinking somebody was going to harm the president. He waved them away, laughing, and said, "What're you doing in my country?" I said, "I've been here two months." He asked, "Where do you live?" I said, "I live in Jamestown," which is the slums of Accra. He shook his head, "You sure must love Africa. How're you getting along?" I said, "I am getting along all right, but the *Pittsburgh Courier* owes me some money. They sent me a check and it bounced." He laughed, and said, "You know what I'm going to do for you?" I said, "What?" He said: "I'm going to put your Harlem behind to work." So, I got a job on this newspaper, the *Evening News*, as the senior reporter at nine pounds a week; that was a good salary then. Man, that was a big salary. Nine pounds a week? The pound was $2.40. My room was one pound and six pence a week, and for three pence you could get enough bananas for a week. You could go to the market and get some local fried fish, and little kids would sell you a bottle of fresh water for three cents. Your whole meal cost you less than twenty-five cents. So nine pounds was a whole lot of money under the circumstances. We were even sending our clothes out to be cleaned; we were living well. I was sharing a small apartment with a Ghanaian named James Kotey, so I was living very good.

I'd made up my mind that I was going to Africa and see what it was like. You will notice that I had skipped my participation in the Second World War and my four years, six months and twenty-six days of military service because that added nothing to my African awareness at all. It was a waste of my time and a distraction. Before I was drafted into the army, my career was getting underway and I was writing historical stories about Africa, and about the Songhay Empire.

In October of 1940, Willis Huggins died. He had performed in a play called "Black Majesty" where he would stand on the stage and lecture, and when he'd come to a great character in African history one of the members of the group would come and act out the character. I acted out many of these characters, and each one I acted out had to be researched. I researched them so well I could remember them. I would go on the stage, and my cheering crew in the audience would applaud. I was a lousy actor, but I was loud. I thought shouting was good acting. I didn't know any better. "But for the reckless darings of Sonni Ali, the Songhay Empire would have spread itself to the border of the great sea. This is now the duty of Abubukam Muhammad Askia the Great," and I would go on and on. This is how I learned so much about African personalities and the Independent Ethiopian Church. I had to research Abraha's speech when he led the Ethiopian Coptic Church out of the embrace of the Coptic Church of Egypt. He said, "We seek no peace from Rome or Greece; with the affairs of Europe we will have nothing to do. In the future we will decide who will be King of Kings, elector of God and reigning Lion of the Tribe of Judah. We will order justice and dispense mercy in the name of the true God and the true religion."

I often wondered why some Black Marxists didn't stand up and have the guts to say, "I am a Marxist and I am Black; and my Marxism is going to come out of my Blackness, out of my Pan-Africanism and out of my Nationalism. If you don't want to take it that way, jump!" Most Black Marxists model their concept of Marxism after the European model and Karl Marx who did not know the cultures of the non-Western world.

My point is that after leaving the army disenchanted, I tried to pick up my career as an Africanist again, and attended the Association for the Study of Afro-American Life and History (ASALH) meetings as often as I could. Walter Fisher, of Morgan State College, was in charge of the meetings; he was so anticommunist, he made up his mind that I would never read a paper during the time of his chairmanship, and I didn't. That lasted for seven years.

Finally, the chairmanship changed and I began to read papers and gain some kind of acceptance. Besides, some of the older members like Charles Wesley, Lawrence Reddick, Lorenzo Greene, Benjamin Quarles, and the late Raymond Pace Alexander, did not know about this, and when they took a hand at it they regretted the fact that I did not tell them before because they would have done something about it. These were the seniors. These were the people I looked up to. These were my senior scholars, the elders in the Association. They did not know what was happening to me. They knew that while I had been a fellow traveller of the Communist Party for fifty years or more, I had never really been a communist, that I was an independent socialist.

I am a Nationalist, and a Pan-Africanist, first and foremost. Nothing takes precedent over my commitment to my people. While I realized that Karl Marx had some interesting things to say, my study of African communalism and African social living taught me that Karl Marx was a Johnny-come-lately and a political opportunist. He had warmed over and was serving the world some political hash that was already old before Europe and Karl Marx were born. Africans had their form of socialism before Europeans had shoes or lived in a house that had a window and did not have to wait for Europe to bring socialism to the world. I'm not knocking their socialism; for them it may be good. As for us, we've got to dig a little deeper and find out what we did. The roots of our socialism must be rooted in the best things that we have done.

In this period after the war, I was beginning to write again, to research again. I had many jobs, but I was poor. I had a lecture job downtown, a little $25.00 gig. I was glad to get it. I was living in a large furnished room on 136th which I insisted on calling a studio because writers and intellectuals don't live in furnished rooms, they live in studios. For my "studio" my rent was $9.75 a week. The $25.00 lecture fee came in handy. A White woman came up to me all syrupy, and almost pouring herself over me said: "Oh, what can I do for you?" I said, "Get me a job!" By the time I got home people had called me, I didn't know who they were. "NBC," they said, "you want to work tonight?" I said, " Oh Jesus! Tomorrow night would be all right." It was a flunky job but it was a job. I was night chief of maintenance; it was a glorified porter's job, but it was a decent job with decent pay. I had never earned $3.75 an hour in my life; I was to work up to $4.75 an hour. I got in the union, and had some benefits. I participated in early television (by supervising the clean-up crew that prepared the stage); I could see the mechanics of early television unfolding. Finally, they began to recognize my efficiency and decided under pressure they would make me one of their window dressing Negroes, and put me up as window dressing in the front office, and gave me a good job. I was then head of the typing pool, and I was doing some clean white-collar jobs; clean and looking good, acting good and efficient because I always do jobs well. Even if I don't like them, I don't let my skill get rusty, because my skill is something I need to survive by, and I don't even do bad jobs badly.

I'd saved up enough money to go to Africa in 1958. When I came back I decided I would write. I had seen the Africa of my dreams. I had not lived in a hotel; I lived with the people. I lived in their homes. I found that you never can understand the culture of people if you've never had breakfast with them. This is better than a rule of thumb; many people become authorities on people, and have never had breakfast with them. While I was in Ghana, among the Ga peo-

ple with whom I lived, there was an English woman
who came into Accra at 10:00 a.m. and left at 3:00
p.m. The most important things culturally that happened to the Ga people happened between the period
when she was not there. I found a custom there that
we need to seriously think about today. If a young
man marries a girl and he does not have enough
money to set up a house with her, she lives with her
family and he comes to see her and have his last meal
of the day with her, spend some personal time with
her, spend time with her children. Then he goes on
over to his house to sleep or to his mother and
father's house, and she stays right there and sleeps
with her parents. Therefore there are no teenage
pregnancies. They are properly married. This could
be a kind of an alternative for us if we want to consider it.

I began to learn some humane things about
the culture of the Ga people and I purposely wanted
to live among them because they were not Akan. I
had studied the Akan people on paper and had developed all kinds of unfavorable opinions of them. Later,
in Ghana, I was to meet Joseph B. Danquah, the
greatest living authority on the Akans during that
time. I was to witness customary court trials. At one
customary court trial, I thought they didn't have
much to consider. A man goofed off and two other
men had to finish his job. The men finished his job
and collected their pay and gave him his share as
though he had worked. Then they passed a bar and
saw him spending the money on women, and setting
up people, and they felt betrayed. They took the matter to their headsman, their king, the subchief under
the Asantehene, who is supreme. The trial lasted
three nights, and I wondered, "What's all the fuss
about? The man promised to give back the money,
he apologized, what's it all about now?" The trial kept

going on. I learned one thing about African customary court trials; the accused can examine everybody
in the court, including the judge. The accused called
his last character witness, his wife. She said, "He is
weak of eyes now, and this situation has given him
the eyes of a child. He is a good man, a good
provider, but sometimes he fancies that he is rich.
He likes to give away things and set people up, and
you know, go to the bars and tell everybody to drink
on him. Otherwise, he takes care of his family. He
doesn't spend so much that there's nothing left for
the family." She defended his honor, and then she
turned to the men to plead for them to work with him
again. The key issue was those same men, must
work with him again in order for him to restore his
faith in himself.

I went to Dr. Danquah, and asked, "Dr.
Danquah, what was the trial about?" Dr. Danquah is
a lawyer and he speaks to everybody. His father was
a school teacher, so he addresses everybody as
though he is a school teacher and they are students.
"John, you're acting like a silly Westerner. Go down
to my library, read this, read this, and read this!"
Then he gave me a little pamphlet, twenty-six pages.
He said, "My wife is preparing dinner; when you find
the answer we will have our dinner." I read and read,
and I finally read that twenty-six-page pamphlet, and
I learned that African society is held together by
honor and obligation. I went upstairs and I said, "Dr.
Danquah, the trial was about the restoration of the
man's honor. He had violated the custom of his people and he had apologized and tried to make amends.
If the men who accused him did not work with him
again, his honor would not have been restored, and
his ability to be obligated to the customs of his people would not have been restored. So honor and
obligation was what the trial was about. It is also

what African life is about.  This is why Africa could
build an enduring society that could last thousands
of years without a jail system."  He said, "John, we
will have our dinner now."  No school could have
taught me that lesson.

Danquah, who had trained Nkrumah and
invited him back to Ghana, was furiously angry with
him at this point.  He never stopped addressing
Nkrumah in the same way he addressed him when
Nkrumah was a school boy, "Francis, stop talking
nonsense!"  His name was Francis K. Nkrumah.
Francis was his Christian name, but Danquah kept
addressing him that way when he was head of state,
and Nkrumah didn't particularly like the idea.  He
said Nkrumah's autobiography, *Ghana*, contains
three factual errors per page.  He sent me down to his
library to read the log books of The United Gold Coast
Convention and to read Nkrumah's autobiography.
Danquah was right.  Factually, it contained an average of three errors per page.  Nkrumah dictated the
autobiography from memory, without any records in
front of him, and he could not correctly recall all
those facts, all those dates, and all those different
people who attended the meetings when he was sec-
retary.  It's an understandable error, but an error, no
doubt.

I returned to America by way of Rome and
Paris, and wanted to write a book about my travels;
no one was interested in publishing it. I had been to
Nigeria, to Ife and Ibadan, and I had seen the leading
intellectuals and the most able people of Nigeria.
Nigeria was on the verge of independence, and I could
see England setting up Nigeria to fall apart.  England
would be successful.  The whole concept of separate
states within Nigeria would put one group against the
other, causing  an internal crisis within Nigeria that
has not been resolved until this day.  The Europeans

forgot one thing which we also seem to have forgotten; the idea of a nation-state is European. The Africans did not have nation-states; they had territorial states, and there is a big difference between the two. Territorial states have no tight borders. This means that the cultural entities in one state can relate to those of the other state because nearly all states are multiethnic in character. This is true of Ghana right now. Some of the cultural states of the Mossi people of Burkina Faso are in northern Ghana. When Burkina Faso has an election, the people from northern Ghana go into Burkina Faso and participate in the election. This is the difference between the territorial state and the nation-state where you cannot cross the border unless you have a passport.

My book about my early travels in West Africa was called *Africa Without Tears*, and it dealt with just what I saw there. I went to the north to see the Akan people; I learned the difference between the Yoruba culture and the Ibo culture. I went to the north of Nigeria to study the Hausa-Fulani people. I tried to talk to women in the dye pits, and get to know the different people, and the different forms of culture in Nigeria. I learned the most from the Akan people in Ghana because I went north and lived in Kumasi for a while, all the time, living among the people and relating to the people. I learned much in my travels from Ghana to Nigeria. I wrote a long piece on it that I'm going to include in a book one day called *Africa To Me*, dealing with my African fascination. The piece will be called "Journey From Accra To Lagos."

On the journey I did not know that bus drivers were paid according to the length of time it takes to make the trip, and that the bus conveniently breaks down at a border check point to lengthen the trip. The bus was broken down when I was going to the border. A little man in a truck stopped. He was a bread delivery man. He had one space in the car for somebody to ride, so he looked at me and said: "Ewe man, come here, come here." I'm not Ewe so I didn't move. "Ewe man, come here!" I came over. "Where you going?" I said, "I'm going to the border." "Get in." He began to talk to me, in Ewe. Rapid Ewe I can't understand, slow Ewe I can. He swore that I was Ewe. I was glad that somebody claimed me. He was complaining that he was a bread delivery man, and that when the bakers were late the women in the market place would shake their fists at him because their trays would be empty and they would have no bread to sell. He said, "Am I a baker? What can I do? Can I tell the bakers when to get the bread ready?" I sympathized with him of course.

He finally delivered the bread and took me ten miles inland, to his headsman, or chief. He explained my dilemma; when they were speaking Ewe so fast and I didn't understand he would say, "This man don't know he's Ewe, poor fellow." The chief settled it. He got ten men, lined them up beside me, and he pointed to my nose and their nose, and told me to look. Their nose was pugged the same as mine, identical. These were Africans I had never seen in my life. He said, "He is our son. He is home. He is welcome. Good-bye." The end of it. I said to myself then, if things get hot for me in the United States I was going to learn Ewe, dress Ewe, speak Ewe, and if I saw any Black Americans in my newly adopted country, which would be Togo, I would say, "I hear you come from a country where they're still lynching and murdering people. I plan to visit one day, if you learn to behave yourself. Never been there myself of course." It is a happening inside of you, it's a spiritual happening to know that there's some place in the world where by physical identity you are accepted as part of a people. No matter what doubt you have, they have no doubt

in their mind that physically you belong to them.
They have told you that you are home, you are welcome; they accept you, and that's the end of it, no
more argument. It's a good feeling. It never happened in any other place.

When I came back to the United States I wrote
my book called *Africa Without Tears*—a corny title. I
would probably change it now; I still have the same
material so I can integrate it into a larger work. My
job had ended, I had earned the money to go to Africa
on the job at NBC. I came back to the job, and I
started writing. Now, I was participating in the
Association meetings a little more. Walter Fisher had
gone back to being the librarian at Morgan State
College, where he should have stayed in the first
place. He was not hounding me anymore. I was still
a fellow traveller, doing better work with the communists than most communists, though not a party
member. I was still arguing with them, still telling
them that Karl Marx was a Johnny-come-lately, and
that socialism was in the world before Europeans
were in the world. I was not having too much suc-
cess with these loggerheads, still kind of regretting all
the time I spent arguing with people who closed down
their minds, but making progress in my search for
Africa. Finally, I was teaching in the community,
doing the best I could, gradually moving up, and
beginning to teach in New York University's
Headstart and Upward Bound programs. As long as
the government was furnishing the money the job
lasted; if the government money ran out, the job was
no more. I married again. I took William Leo
Hansberry to the New School For Social Research for
a series of lectures; these were very treasured lectures. I taped all of these and somebody borrowed
the tapes to make a copy, and pretended that they
lost them, or that they were stolen. They were stolen

all right, stolen from me.

Hansberry lectured at the New School For Social Research. My acquaintance with him deepened my understanding of African Studies. I was acquainted with him as part of the audience when he lectured, but now I got to know him personally. He was a great scholar, and a very shy human being with very little fight in him. I participated in the American Society for African Culture, that brought Africans to visit America. Now, I was beginning to become acquainted with Africans of the Francophone community and the Anglophone community.

I met Alioune Diop while stopping over in Paris on my way home from Africa. We remained friends until he died only a few years ago. When he came to America, I was the one he thought would understand the importance of African culture. I wrote my first article for *Presence Africaine* on my way home from my African trip. I called it "Wake Keeping Among the Ga People of Ghana" but it was published under the title "The Celebration of a Wake Among the Ga People." The number of articles I had written about my travels in Africa also included "Third Class on the Blue Train to Kumasi," "The Morning Train to Ibadan," and "A Journey from Accra to Lagos," which was the longest of the many articles.

My acquaintance with Alioune Diop would lead to my acquaintance with other historians, including Father Eckelbert Mvane. I could not attend the first International Congress of Africanists in Accra in 1961, being broke and newly married, and paying the expenses thereof. I did attend the second conference in Dakar. I had heard of Cheikh Anta Diop and had several of his books in French along with their rough translations. I borrowed one of the translators at the conference, a girl named Jeannette Stovall, and we went to Dr. Diop's office and laboratory. He not only greeted me kindly but sent his son out to get the new books he had written that I had not seen. We became friends from that moment and stayed friends until he died. We were very close. My twenty year relationship with this man was one of the treasured things in my life.

Now, the Civil Rights Movement was spilling over into other dimensions. African Americans were beginning to demand more than just civil rights; they were beginning to demand a look at their history from an African point of view. I attended the 1968 conference of the African Studies Association in Los Angeles. We called a caucus. Dr. Len Jeffries, then at San Jose University, Cheke Unwache, Shelby Smith, and quite a few others called this conference, and we decided to form an organization of our own. Later on in 1968 we met at Federal City University in Washington, D.C. and began to program the organization. I was reluctant to accept any responsibility beyond that of being an active member, but I eventually accepted the presidency. In a large meeting at Howard University, after the cleavage at the African Studies Association Conference in Montreal in 1969, over two thousand people attended, and the organization really came into being. Some of the most able people of the African world were present.

The African Heritage Studies Association (AHSA) came into being concurrent with the demand for Black Studies throughout the country. I could see then where we were going wrong. We were going wrong even in demanding Black Studies; we made the mistake that we are still making. Black Studies is not a separate entity; we are talking about the missing pages in the history of the world. We are talking not only about the cheating of Black students of information they need in the world of tomorrow, we are talking about the cheating of White students also, because in the world of tomorrow both White students and Black students will have to look at each other from a different point of view than previously, with a different set of information. It's just as valuable to them as it is to us, because in the world of tomorrow they will be dealing with African people from different perspectives.

African people will learn something that they have not learned today—that they are not learning in South Africa, they are not learning in Namibia—and that is that Europeans never share power. There's no place where the Europeans ever shared power with anyone. Europeans came out with one mission in mind—to control. They have always solved their problems at the expense of the people outside of Europe. I think we're going to ultimately have to do what Arthur Schomburg taught me that first day we met during his lunch hour; we might have to step backwards in order to step forward. We might have to study Europe's relationship to us in order to understand something of the disruptive relationship that we have with ourselves. We might have to accept some responsibility we never dreamed about, and that is the responsibility of the restoration of humanity to the world.

If you ask me what we owe our oppressor, I can answer easily: Nothing. Yet, part of your mission to rescue yourself is going to be ironically a mission to rescue him, too, because he is a part of the world. I'm not copping out into nonviolence because I don't believe in nonviolence. I believe in it as a strategy only. I do not believe in it as a way of life. If you're going to restore humanity to world, you've got to fight for a restoration of the humanity to the world, you've got to fight for a restoration of the humanity of all people. You should have no illusions about Asians liking you. Some of them have the same stereotype concepts of you that Whites have. You should have no illusions about the Japanese having a solution for you. They form solutions to meet their needs. What we're going to have to do is to reclaim those things that belong to us, and we have to prepare for it. We must develop a temperament for freedom, and we must learn some lessons from history that lead to our liberation. We must locate ourselves on the maps of human geography. Between the Caribbean Islands, South America, and the United States, there may be up to two-hundred million African people in the Western hemisphere. There are millions of African people in India—almost a hundred-million—and millions in the Pacific. The population in Africa has been counted as five-hundred-million for the last fifty years. We might go into the twenty-first century with a billion African people on the face of this earth. We must stop being cultist consumers and become producers of some of the things we wear, and some of the things we eat.

We must listen to some of our messengers that we've misunderstood. Booker T. Washington had something to say, but not all things to say. W.E.B. DuBois had something to say, but not everything to say. Understanding Booker T. Washington would have logically led you to understand his program of economic self-reliance, which would have logically led you to DuBois' program of political self-reliance, and that would have logically led you to Marcus Garvey's program of the reclamation and the redemption of Africa. From that you would have understood Malcolm X and Elijah Muhammad's ideas about the lost nation of African people away from home. African people away from home have gained some skills and technical knowledge for working in partnership with Africans on the continent, to contribute to African development.

I think somewhere in misunderstanding Africa, and misunderstanding the mission of Black Studies, we went down the road, and we took the same wrong turn. We saw some forks in the road, some roads leading in different directions, and we didn't read the sign boards as well as we needed to.

We have to come back to the fork in the road, and read those sign boards again. I do not choose to call it Black Studies because it's really Africana Studies, that is probably the best word for it, because Africana Studies embraces all Africans—those in African America, the Caribbean, Africa itself, in the Pacific, and in Asia. We might as well get in the habit of calling it Africana Studies. Once we understand this, we have to understand that history is a clock that people use to tell their political and cultural time of day. It is also a compass that people use to locate themselves on the map of human geography. History tells you where you have been, and what you have been. It tells you what you are, and where you are. Most importantly, history tells you where you still must go, and what you still must be. My serious study of African people has taught me that the relationship of a people to their history is the same as the relationship of a mother to her child.

# PART II

POST–WORLD WAR II YEARS

# POST–WORLD WAR II YEARS

Many Western-educated Africans have been brain-washed into believing that Africa has no answer for Africa's problems. Africans have to develop their own solutions for Africa's problems, because Europe has no answer. As far as we are concerned, the European interpretation of both communism and capitalism is a failure. And the European interpretation of democracy and Christianity is also a failure.

I did not say that these things are failures across the board, I said that the European has announced these things to the world, but he attaches importance to none of them; and he violated them most in relationship to us. In relationship to us, he has violated all of them. He has already proved that he is totally incapable of understanding any of them, and that he does not have the temperament to live by any of them. Yet, we are following behind him as though we believe what he's saying. We have developed a habit of following people who don't know where they are going; because we want to be like other people. We live with the illusion that we're just like other people, we're just as good as other people. That's not what you need to prove. Maybe your salvation might be that you are not like other people. Maybe your salvation might be that you came out of a society that had a humanity different from that of other people. I don't accept ideas of cultural superiority and inferiority. I deal with cultural variances, cultural infusion and diffusion.

For example, many students are convinced that what Booker T. Washington was doing was nega-

tion, and that the difference of opinion between
Booker T. Washington and W.E.B. DuBois was a
fight. Booker T. Washington was an agrarian, serving
a white man whom he had never seen. His mother
had been a slave. Agrarian means a farming,
Southern background. He had to work his way partly through school. W.E.B. DuBois was a New
England petty aristocrat. In New England, you could
be an aristocrat without having money if you had a
good family, good status, good manners, if you went
to church, and you had not disgraced yourself. You
established your class status by virtue of good con-
duct, and by virtue of association. W.E.B. DuBois
grew up in New England where he came from a
socialist town—I mean socialist in the popular sense
now, not socialist in the communist revolutionary
sense which is a fake anyhow, but that's another lecture—a town where the leading young men, upon fin-
ishing high school, were sent to Harvard at the
expense of the town. He was one of them, and he
assumed he would go to Harvard. Harvard was an
academic heaven. I know a Black professor at
Harvard right now who thinks Harvard is so precious,
he said if Harvard burns down he will attend the
ashes. The stamp of Harvard is still valued, and we
still don't know there are schools in America where
you can get a better education than at Harvard. With
all of its formalism, Harvard was founded to do what
this nation was founded to do; it was founded for free
White Protestant males, middle-class and up, those
who agree with the prevailing political status quo,
and those who own property. The most valuable
property then was slaves.

If you have the illusion that all Americans were
supposed to enjoy democracy, then you have misread
this. Not only were all Americans not supposed to
enjoy it, but the White woman wasn't supposed to

enjoy it either; she got the vote, day before yesterday, in 1920. After all of the suffragist movements, all of the tricks of the movements, and all of Susan B. Anthony's antics, she didn't get the vote until she finally said to the White man, "In a country where no White women can vote, some Black men *can* vote." She got the vote on the backs of Black men. To a large extent, her affirmative action right now is being achieved by taking jobs from Black men and giving these jobs to White women.

People do not understand the trials and tribulations that are heaped on Black men and women, and they also do not understand the European mentality. Europe traditionally solves its problems outside of Europe, and the Europeans are geniuses at draining the diseased pus of their political sores on the lands of other people.

If you understand what I am saying, then you understand what is happening in South Africa right now. When the problem of Europe's Middle Ages— famine, poor people, poor land and poor resources— was solved, it was solved by the slave trade. Solved at our expense. Once more, Europe is solving its economic problems by holding on to the gold and the diamonds in Africa; holding on to the resources of Africa, and again the left is no different from the right in this regard.

The movies have geared your mind to think that there is a good guy and a bad guy in every drama, but there are dramas in the world with no good guys and there are dramas in the world with two good guys. This is why you don't understand the difference between DuBois and Washington. You have a drama where you are choosing right and wrong, but on proper examination both men were right. They were both right. It wasn't a question of DuBois or Booker T. Washington. It was the same answer then as now; DuBois and Booker T. Washington. Washington for industrial preparation and self-reliance, DuBois for political consolidation.

If you understand that, you will understand how logically the political conveyor belt led from Booker T. Washington to DuBois, from DuBois to Garvey. If you understand all of this, you will understand—in spite of whether you want to be a Muslim or not—that Garvey would logically lead you to a consideration of what Elijah Muhammad and Malcolm X were saying. Nation reclamation: all of them were talking about the same thing using different words. They would also lead to the examination of the two major radical journalists, T. Thomas Fortune, and William Monroe Trotter, and the major Black woman journalist, Ida. B. Wells. One thing about history is that if you open one door, ten other doors open. This is why when people come and ask me what is 'the book' on the subject, I say there is no 'the book' on any subject. There is no final book on any subject. There are certain books on subjects that are better than other books on the subject, and there are some books that will set your mind in motion and lead you to other books on the subject.

Had we followed Booker T. Washington's industrial education, you wouldn't see a White plumber in a Black neighborhood. Plumbers make more money than college presidents. A man who lays tiles in a bathroom, and lays it well, makes more money than a tenured professor. (A tenured professor has a hard time hiring one of them.) Washington was saying, to become skillful at those jobs where you use your mind and your hands well. If you live in a brick house, what's wrong with owning a brick yard? I recall a story of a young man who walked across three states to get to Tuskegee. He arrived at Tuskegee bare-footed, because he had worn out his shoes. He began a shoe repair shop at Tuskegee. Later, he opened a school to train young men to make general shoes, and orthopedic shoes; most of the Blacks who went into making corrective shoes were trained at Tuskegee. Its cooking and baking schools were so good that the Army sent their cooks to Tuskegee to be trained.

When I was a master sergeant in the Army, I inherited the last of those great cooks from Tuskegee, a little man named Slaughter. I don't know what Slaughter weighed . . . if you wet him down he might have weighed 110 pounds, but he could cook! I defy you to taste one of his biscuits and leave them alone. He'd go all out. If I'm permitted an aside, I had a girl-friend I wanted to spoil, so I invited her to eat in our mess hall. I took sheets from the supply room, and everybody ate on 'table cloths' that day. I asked Slaughter to bake her a cake. When he came to me he says, "So"—he's a slow talking Southerner, like most of us Southerners—he says, "Sarge, you didn't tell me what kind of cake your lady likes, so I cooked three. I hope she likes one of them." Bless his soul wherever he is! Whenever I had a troop train with a kitchen, I would take Slaughter. What I'm saying is that Tuskegee sent forth into our community our first printers, and our first people who had shoe repair shops, etc. You can't just toss Booker T. Washington off.

In a course I taught here at the Africana Studies and Research Center some years ago on "Men and Movements in the Black Urban Ghetto," I devoted a session to Booker T. Washington. I began by saying to the students, "If anybody calls Booker T. Washington 'Uncle Tom' there are two doors leading out of this classroom. I want you to use one of them." This came from someone who takes pride in the fact that the students don't even have to make appoint-

ments with me.   They know where I am; they can
walk right up to me and say what they want to say.
I'm available; when I'm available, I'm totally available.
        As I explained to the class, Booker T.
Washington was a strategist whose strategy often did
not work.   He did not take a stand on many things;
no public stand against lynching, no public stand
against the famous race riot in 1906. There are four-
teen volumes of his letters; I have them, and I have
read them.   This man was against lynching and he
was devastating in the way he attacked people for not
showing their public duty in defense of Black people.
He was also a schizophrenic.   I maintain that Black
people can't even afford to be schizophrenic. We live
in a society where pressure is so hard on us, we have
to be 'multi-phrenics.' You need six personalities just
to survive as Black people.   Two personalities just
won't do.  We can't even get through the day with just
two personalities. We have to have a whole bag of
masks and put them on when necessary.   If you see
a particular individual coming, you put the appropri-
ate mask on.  We choose what mask we're going to
put on to cover our real self.
        Let's go back to this African who said that he
didn't think that African socialism could fit into the
Africa of today.  He's dead wrong.  No society remains
static, and there's nothing in the European Middle
Ages that the Europeans can use today in quite the
same way. Systems of government grow like people;
things become obsolete.   Many things that worked
well one time, won't work well the next time.   Years
ago we lived in the country; if Grandma came to visit
or if the house became crowded, we called in six men
and added a room to the house.   Today, building is
expensive; labor is expensive; we can't do that anymore.   Besides, we live in apartments now.   That's
static.  Our way of life has kept us from doing many

of the humane things we used to do. We used to traditionally invite people over for Sunday dinner; we
had a lot of dinner then.  Food was cheaper, and
those great cooks that traditionally came out of our
society would put things together; now those great
cooks aren't there anymore and who's supposed to be
the cook will just send you to Kentucky Fried. That
doesn't mean we're not hospitable anymore. It means
that there were certain facilities we had, certain times
we had during that period, that we do not have now.

   Now, to move to the main theme of today's lecture, I will go back to 1969, when I first came to
Cornell's newly-established Africana Studies and
Research Center.  I was here doing a summer con-
sultancy for teachers. Jackie Haskins, who later
became James Turner's assistant, came to me and
said, "James wants to see you about something. He's
coming to the Center and wants to know if you're
interested in teaching a course," and I said, "Of
course, yes I would."  Really, she is the one who did
the recruiting and kept in touch for him, before he
came to the Center.  Soon after I began teaching at
the Center, some local Ku Klux Klansmen burned it
down, along with some of my books and some other
people's books.  We had to board in one of the newer
buildings on campus and later moved back to the
Center.  The stimulating thing about that period is
that I was going to Hunter College at the same time,
building the Department of Black and Puerto Rican
Studies, and the department was brand new. No one
had an idea of what the department should be, and I
took full advantage of that and fashioned the department the way I thought it should be.  It wasn't a bad
department, and I recently said that it was the number one Black Studies program in the country until I
left, then the Africana Center took over.  I was very
bold in saying it because I always announced that

Hunter was the number one, Africana Center was second, and I was very proud to have an association with both of them. I would classify them according to what most of my work happened to be. Coming here and finding students so alert was one of the best, and most stimulating, teaching experiences of my life.

I found students who had left other schools. One student had been thrown out of N.Y.U. because a professor disputed her paper on the racial origins of the last Seminole War. Osceola, Chief of the Seminole Indians of Florida, had a Black wife, an escaped slave whom the Whites tried to reclaim. He had a Seminole Indian army and also a Black army of escaped slaves. These two combined armies of Indians, and mainly the Blacks, fought so well that an American officer fighting them said that these are not Indian wars, these are "nigger wars."  We need to study the Seminole Wars and our relationship with the Seminole Indians, and with the so-called Indians, because in the first place that was not what they were. Christopher Columbus gave them that name, and Christopher Columbus was a faker.  He started off in search of the East Indies.  He ended up in the West Indies and slapped the  word "Indians" on a people.

These people were Caribs and Arawaks.  He destroyed the greater portion of them.  Lerone Bennett has a good chapter on this—about the third chapter in a book called *The Shaping Of Black America*—dealing with Black and Indian relationships.  A man named Kenneth Porter has written an entire book on this subject.  There's plenty of material on this subject so we need not push that any further.  The student told me that she wanted to extend her research, and wanted to know if she would cause any problems with me by writing such a paper.  I said, "You will have no problem with me, you will endear yourself to me if you just dig deeper. Let's see what else you come up with. Go as far as your mind will take you." She finished here and to make it short, she got a Ph.D., did an excellent dissertation on slavery in Virginia, and the last time I saw her she was teaching in Dayton, Ohio.

That's one of the many students I taught at Cornell. There's another student I remember. Cornell was recruiting people from the so-called ghetto, and one of them got a scholarship. She sat in the front row and wore a little cap for some reason. I could never tell whether she was smirking or smiling. She never asked any questions, she never participated in discussion. Near the end of the semester, she came into my office and said, "Professor Clarke, you think because I don't say anything, I don't dig you. I dig you, you're an all right cat. Come paper time, I'm gonna lay one on you." At the end of the semester, she came to my office. Her little cap on, same kind of smirk or smile on her face. She said, "You have talked about David Walker's *Appeal*. You've talked about it sociologically, historically and otherwise, but you missed the main point. You have not talked about it astrologically. Under what sign was this man born?" I said, "Oh-oh!" She entered an area about which I not only knew nothing, but didn't even care. People tell me, "You were born under the sign of this." My daughter says, "You belong under this sign, this is why you are so mean." I said, "Yeah, yeah, yeah, you go to bed, you clean your room; don't tell me about signs." [The student] threw the paper on the desk and turned to leave the office. I read the paper immediately. It was so well written and, interestingly, I did something that I had never previously done in my professional life. I reached across my desk, picked up my red pencil and put an "A" on the paper before I had finished reading it. It was that good.

I was here when Ann Kelley attended; she was another brilliant student among the many who attended this school. Another student from Chicago wrote a book based on her master's thesis on the spirituals. She is the only student that I know who, unfortunately, has passed on since then. Teaching here was an experience that was both rewarding and stimulating.

Mohawk Airlines, which I used to come to Ithaca at that time, didn't always run on schedule, so we called it "Slow Hawk." They used those old Fairchild airplanes, and they did get you there, even if they did not get you there on time. They had a strike, so I had to fly into Syracuse and take a bus into Ithaca. It was about as cold as it could be, and yet there was a stimulation drawing me here to teach. They were the best years that I have enjoyed during my teaching life. I still have most of those papers, including, some place in my file, the paper of the little girl who wore the cap. I began something which I would continue throughout my entire teaching life, giving out extensive notes for every class, with references and page numbers where to find the references. Someone said that I was spoon-feeding the students. "You didn't leave them enough things to do." What I started them to do was research in areas they had never dreamed about. I introduced them to subject matters that they'd never given any thought to. This had been my training outside of college because I was self-trained; I didn't just read the prescribed books. I also read the unprescribed books. I read the radical books; I read the dissenting books. I had the range of information over and above the regular academically trained person.

In the meantime, I had gotten my classes under way at Hunter College. The Black and Puerto

Rican students who brought me there were now con-
fronting me that first year. I found that some of them
were really not that serious. They had brought me
there to build a Black Studies program for political
reasons, but they had no intention of seriously studying it. Some of them didn't even come to the classes.
Finally, they confronted me and said, "You know, we
brought you here, we voted, and we told the school
either bring a person like you here or we'll tear the
school down. You're working us harder than whitey."
I told them:

> That is because I love you more. I know
> more than whitey what you're going to have
> to face out there, and I'm preparing you to
> face it. I'm not only going to prepare you to
> face it academically, I am preparing you to
> face it ideologically. You must understand
> that the world out there wasn't shaped for
> you, it was shaped by the European for the
> European. For five hundred years, the
> world has been shaped to suit European
> people. They shape everything and you
> have to understand how to get through all
> of that and be what you need to be.

Already I had been introduced to the work of
Basil Davidson, an able Englishman. I already knew
the work of the great master Black writers on the
subject. In the old Harlem History Club, I had been
introduced to the work of Gerald Massey, his six-volume work dealing with how Christianity was stolen
out of Egypt. This was before Dr. ben-Jochannan
and I had established a relationship. We had met,
but we had no day by day relationship. When we
finally met again, we started an argument we haven't
settled to this day. The reason we don't settle the
argument is because we like it. I said the Eighteenth
Pharaonic Dynasty was the greatest dynasty to ever

sit on any throne, at anytime, in the history of all the world.  He said, "Man you must be crazy, it is the nineteenth.  You got to examine Ramses."  He sticks to the nineteenth, I stick to the eighteenth.  When I praised Cleopatra he said, "You're praising somebody that was a half-breed who slept around with a bunch of Romans."

I claim Cleopatra because, whatever she was, mixed or not mixed, she was an African nationalist. She manipulated Caesar and Anthony, and kept the worst aspect of Roman rule from the backs of her people.  I don't think she loved or liked either one of them; however on her death bed, she said, "I will now join my father, the sun."  No Greek woman would have said that; her statement came from an African belief system.  Greek women were not worshipping Amen-Ra at that time; Greek women were not worshipping Gods who related to the sun.  This woman was an African nationalist.  She was also a teenage politician, more brilliant than some of the politicians that we have today, and she did more with it.  Maybe she did have to bargain with her charms in and out of bed.  If that is true, I don't know anybody who got more for it.  Dr. ben-Jochannan would have said she was a slut.  We crossed swords then, but we love each other like brothers, and we look after each other like brothers.

Among the living people around me, he's about as close to me as any brother I've ever had.  Yet we have some strong intellectual disagreements.  He made a cult out of the study of Nile River Civilizations.  I studied the civilizations of the other rivers of Africa, starting with the Niger, and how these civilizations related to Egypt and the Nile Valley civilizations.  I also studied the area of the Sahara before it became a desert.  I studied the indentations in the earth that showed where rivers used to be in the

Sahara. There was once a cluster of great cities in this part of Africa. Henri Lhote's book, *The Search for the Tassilli Frescoes*, documents this, and recent archaeological digs reaffirm his claims. We need to reconsider other areas in Africa that fed the Nile. We have to reconsider the south as the mother of the Nile and as the mother of Egyptian civilization. We need to reconsider Egypt before the Greeks gave it that name—the ancient Africans never called it Egypt. Dr. (ben-Jochannan) and I are very supportive of each other, in many different ways, and we are committed one to the other. I don't assume that the Nile is all he knows, but I know that the Nile is his great love in Africa. Yet if you push him the right way, Dr. ben knows more about treaties—the broken treaties, especially the Berlin conferences. He knows more detail than almost any man I know. He's got a good general knowledge of all of Africa, but his particular specialty, his particular love is that Nile Valley.

It's mine too, but my main focus is the Niger, and the other river civilizations of Africa. For example, the Limpopo, which is an East African civilization between the Limpopo and the Zambezi; the Volta River civilization is in the area now called Burkina Faso. Also, the Congo River civilization, especially the period when the people of the Congo drove the Portuguese out, in the 1590s, and remained free until 1884. It is one of the great miracles in African history because it happened in the midst of the slave trade and the colonial period. I like to think of myself as a generalist in relationship to Africa, rather than a specialist on any one part of it, and there are some parts I know better than some other parts.

During that period, having worked for NBC, I wrote a serial, a series of articles, and a book that was never published, *Lives of Great African Chiefs*, about African kings of the resistance move-

ment.    It was published in serial form in the
*Pittsburgh Courier* between 1957 and 1958.    The
series lasted six months.    I was always active, and
when the McCarthy period came along, driving people
out of work, many people were crying; but I did not
cry.    I had a job.    I worked at night and wrote in the
day.    I wasn't afraid to do menial work, and I would
work from a menial job up to an administrative job.    I
wasn't afraid to start any place.    I wasn't afraid to
clerk in auto-laundries.    I wasn't afraid to do whatsoever I had to do in order to survive, and being a good
cook, naturally I didn't starve.

I did not absent myself from the ladies either.
I departmentalized life: so much for studies, so much
for the ladies, so much for work.    This is a very intel-
ligent way to handle it.    I wasn't a fool, I wasn't crazy.
Most of the ladies related to the organizations I
belonged to.    By now, the clash between ASA (African
Studies Association) and AHSA (African Heritage
Studies Association) became wide and permanent.
The first conference of the International Congress of
Africanists was held in Accra in 1961.    I could not go.
I was newly married with a new baby, and I didn't
have the funds to go.    Everybody not only assumed
that I would be there, but put me on the program in
two places.    They assumed that I would automatical-
ly be there, but no one made any provision to get me
there.    Fortunately, Julian Mayfield, who would later
teach here at the Africana Center for a while, was
editing documents in Ghana at the time, and he sent
me all of the papers.    I got a complete set of every
paper—not the edited papers, but the complete
papers—including some submitted but not delivered.
That's one of the good things my old friend did for me,
partly in compensation for all the books he borrowed
from me and never returned.    He was notorious for
borrowing books and notorious for not returning

them, including some of the documents I had collected in Ghana during my stay.

Now, teaching at the Center, and teaching at Hunter, I'm getting public recognition I never got before. While I was here at the Center, a reporter from the *New York Times* wrote a very good article on me. Hunter wanted to know, "Inasmuch as your main salary is here, this is your full-time job. This is where you're going to get your pension if you stay long enough; we're the one giving you health services and you're only adjunct over there. Why did they give you so much publicity for being at the Africana Center and didn't even mention that you were also here at Hunter College?" I smoothed that over by saying that the interviewer contacted a whole lot of people who didn't even know that I was at Hunter College. He just interviewed me briefly; then he interviewed other people to see what I was doing here. That went over, although that wasn't the complete truth; the complete truth of the matter was that I was so centralized, I was so concentrated here at the Center, I didn't give a thought to the fact that I was also at Hunter. It also gave me some public attention that I needed, and both my friends and my enemies would make good use of it. Many people think that if you get in the *New York Times* you have to be a sellout, you must be a pawn of the CIA, or FBI or something like that; that was not true in my case.

During the same time, Blacks and sharecroppers were living in tents after having been put off their land in Alabama. I was now at the Anti-Poverty Program in Harlem, where I stayed for five years as head of the Heritage Teaching Program. No one knew what I was teaching, or cared to know that what the Anti-Poverty hustlers were interested in was their middle-class salaries; they forgot the Anti-Poverty Program was developed to relieve people of poverty. It

relieved them of theirs, and they weren't too worried
if it didn't relieve any one else. To that extent it was
a sham, so I helped to develop something called the
Community Action Institute, and, had it developed
with some kind of cooperation, Harlem would have
become a more important political factor in New York
City; one to be reckoned with. We forget to recognize
the significance of the Jewish vote because the
Jewish vote is tightly organized and Jewish money is
tightly organized. Few people know that all the Jews
in the world are less than one half of the Black population in the United States, and Israel gets more aid
than all the African countries in the world put together. They have their political thing together, but we
don't have ours together.

I was to deliver a lecture in New Orleans at the
American Historical Association meeting, called the
"Myth Of Black Anti-Semitism." In this lecture, I laid
out how and proved that Black people always had a
sentimental attachment to Jewish people, because
during slavery we wanted to attach ourselves to a
people who had escaped from something. Our psy-
chological out was to make the Exodus real, so the
Exodus became more meaningful to us than to them.
We wept about the three Hebrew boys in the fiery fur-
nace. See, but we're still hung-up on the myth that
everything in the Bible is supposed to be true and the
inspired word of God; we're still hung-up on that one.

A few years ago, I was visiting my sister in her
home in Georgia. She's one of the people who loves
me with much passion and attention. Her Jesus
dependency is so thick that three days at her home is
about as much as I can take at one time. She'd pray
for me in the morning, pray for me in the evening,
and God's supposed to be doing everything. Take
your word to the Lord and leave it there.

There was a T.V. series called "The Bible." The episode I saw dealt with the Cain and Abel story, and my sister came out to look at it.

> She was cooking a special meal for me, and she said, "Poor boy, why did he have to kill his little brother like that?" I said, "Oh-oh." I pointed out to her that this was a tropical setting and the characters were wearing tropical clothes, so it couldn't be in Europe; so why were they White? She said, "Now you know it came out of the Bible, and it's God's inspired word; you are not supposed to dispute that." Then she called me by my family nickname, Bubba. She said, "Bubba, you know that's the word of God." I said, "Thank you. Very sorry I interrupted you cooking your meal, you can go back . . ." I knew I'd lost that one. I will never be able to convince her anyway.

I'm going to love her till I die, and she's going to love me till she dies, but I am never going to change her. I'm going to have to take her the way she is, and she's going to try to take me the way I am. She said, "You went up North and read all those books, and forgot all of these things." She has all of my books lined up on the shelf, and she brings her friends in from her choir meetings and shows them the books her brother wrote and edited. She tells her visitors, "Don't put your finger prints on these books now, don't get them dirty." I said, "Please get them dirty. Wear one out by reading it; I can give you another one. Books are supposed to be read." She hasn't read one word, and yet she is as proud as she can be.

She is a remarkable woman; she swore that she would be the last of the females in our family to

work as a servant in the White people's kitchen, and
she kept her promise. She had been a domestic most
of her life, and one of those rural domestics. She did
whatever she had to do, and every one of her children
became successful outside of domestic labor. Her
oldest daughter was manager of a ladies dress store,
and her oldest son is a correctional officer; her other
son is sick now, but before he got hurt in an auto-
mobile accident, he was supervisor of a place where
they make package candy for the vending machines.
Her second daughter is assistant principal in Dublin,
Georgia, working on her Ph.D. in education during
the summer. My sister proved her point; she is the
last of the domestics in our family. She's not
ashamed; she's not apologetic. She trained her children to make their living doing something other than
taking care of White people's clothing, taking care of
White people's children, and taking care of their
houses.

What's this got to do with the subject? It has
to do with my growth and my relationships because I
never broke my relationships with most of my family.
My oldest sister went to California and married a
Mexican, and ran a series of Mexican restaurants;
she then went to Mexico. I think she must have died
there, inasmuch as I never could locate her again.
My other brother went to Detroit, and he was one of
those hustlers around Julian Black, and Roxbury,
one of those hustlers that used to manage Joe Louis.
After they came out of jail, they gave him a piece of
one of their parcels of real estate to manage, because
he had managed to save their property for them during their time in jail. He moved to the suburbs of
Detroit, and I haven't been able to find him. He had
an argument with my stepmother, which he never
forgave us for, nor did he forgive my father for letting
her mistreat the children of my natural mother,

whom all of us worshiped and loved so.

In the seventies, there was a great leap forward. I began to belong to some international organizations, some international associations, and began to attend certain meetings in various places abroad. Fortunately, I knew Tilden LeMelle, and he was in Denver. When I went out to Denver and saw him playing tennis and living almost like a country club professor, I said, "Man, don't you want to come back East and go to work?" He said, "Yes, my wife's sister lives in the East and she wants to go back to be near her sister." So I asked him to come to Hunter College because it was time for me to become chairman, something I didn't want to do because I'm a classroom teacher. I brought him to Hunter because I knew the departing chairman wanted to go back to the English department. LeMelle eventually became chairman and stayed chairman for eight years. These were my best teaching years because I was not only free to travel without missing my classes, I could concentrate on teaching without worrying about administration. When he needed help from me, he got it. I didn't have to worry about filling out all of those forms, and answering all of those letters, and worrying about salary lines and adjunct lines, and all of that. I was free to teach.

I was now exploring a new methodology of teaching. I was doing the same thing in my last year here at the Center, developing basic detailed curriculum at Hunter for the three courses that I taught. I nearly taught African History I and II, and every second semester, I taught a new course, entitled "Men and Movements." I also taught "African Resistance in the Nineteenth Century." I had about four different courses I could switch between. Every second semester I taught a different course during the spring semester. It was a good academic thing for me.

I knew that the partnership between the
Blacks and the Puerto Ricans was not working as
well as I had hoped it would. I pointed out a case in
San Antonio, Texas, where the Mexican numbers
man and the Black numbers man paid the poll tax for
the Blacks and the Mexicans, and they had thirty
thousand votes in their hands. They literally made
the difference in who would become mayor of that
town, and that town became one of the better towns
for Black people in the South. When they integrated
the schools, they had the most intelligent integration
of any town in the South. They integrated the teachers, and they partly integrated the curriculum. It was
done smoothly because they had the churches relating to each other: Whites and Blacks and Mexicans.
The Mexicans and the Blacks didn't marry each
other, and did not have to love each other; but when
it came to voting, they voted in a bloc, and realized
that there had to be a political meeting between them
even if there was no social meeting.

This is where a whole lot of us are misguided
right now. We think integration means you've got to
go to bed with somebody. Integration does not mean
intersexual; integration does not mean that you still
can't have Black preference; and integration does not
mean you have to stop eating corn bread. The
NAACP has done some good radical work, and posi-
tive work in housing, and in law suits, and I don't
want to take it away from them. However, they did
not develop an ideology for integration that was real-
istic. I went to Montgomery during the bus boycott,
and I met Dr. King. He was angry about certain articles that had appeared in the *Pittsburgh Courier*. I
was then working for the *Pittsburgh Courier*, intermit-
tently, because no one ever made a living working for
a Black newspaper. I had to hold down other jobs in
order to keep body and soul together, and I did write

that long series on Africa that I turned into a book manuscript. I was told, "You have proven your point, only we don't choose to pay you for having done so. So we are returning your book."

The book is still unpublished. Only now I would never call the book *The Lives of Great African Chiefs.* I now know the word chief was invented to keep from referring to Africans as kings, a title that would equate them with European kings. Yet, I was dealing with African kings, whose royal lineage goes back a thousand years before the oldest lineage in Europe. If there were any kings in the world, these were kings in the true sense, but no one wanted to recognize this. I wrote about the entire Zulu line, from Chaka to Bimbata who led the last Zulu war. I dealt with the Ashanti wars in West Africa and Yaa Asantewaa, who led the last Ashanti war in 1900. I dealt with the great African Moslem generals. I dealt with Osei Tutu who led the resistance movements early in the eighteenth century. The Blacks who are Moslems today are not ready to deal with the great Black Moslems in Africa, who were not Arabs. What is called Islam among Blacks is Arabism. They do not make a distinction between the two. Arabs have often misused Islam as much as Europeans have often misused Christianity. It is important to recall that the Arab slave trade drained Africa of much energy and much organization. It came a thousand years before the European slave trade, and Africa did not have the energy or the organization to stop the European slave trade. Besides, Africa did not suspect that the Arab stranger and the European stranger were conquerors and slavetraders. Africans, even then, were hospitable to strangers. Africans are hospitable to strangers and still will invite strangers to dinner, even now.

What I'm trying to say is that these are the

kinds of things I took up in the classrooms. The kind
of exploration teaching that had not been done
before. I'd deal with the thousand years before slavery, the independent West African states, other than
Ghana, Mali, and Songhay. I'd deal with what set
this whole idea in motion. I'd deal with the Africans
in Spain and the role they played in Spain. I'd deal
with the fact, which is documented in J.C. DeGraft's
book *African Glory*, that the Africans were in Spain
fifty years before the Arab's arrival. The conquest of
Spain was purely an African conquest. I'd deal with
the early works of John Jackson, especially the chapter in his book, *An Introduction to African Civilization*,
called "Africa: The Civilizing Of Europe," dealing with
the African role in Spain. In the classroom, I'd deal
with the Grandees, the Jews in Spain, who were the
money managers of Spain before it started whitening
itself up. Spain wanted to expel the Arabs, wanted to
expel the Africans, wanted to expel the Jews, and
they did all of that. If it was whitening itself up in
expelling the Jews, then what color were the Jews?
These were the Sepharadic Jews, the East African
and the Western Asian Jews. I don't use the word
Middle East because I don't know the Middle from
Western Asian Jews. These were the Jews who are
second-class citizens in Israel, right now.

The Jews would not deal with their Black com-
ponents. They would not deal with the migration of
the Jews after the Roman dispersion of their temple
in 70 A.D. Many of them went down into Africa. The
idea of teaching is to open doors that had been
closed, and to call attention to books well written, but
not read. For example, Father William's account of
*Hebrewisms of West Africa*, where he traces the
Hebrew elements in African civilizations, and how
they got there. That Hebrew element was brought in
with Western Asian Jews. With the dispersion of the

Jews by the Romans, many of these Jews went to live in inner West Africa. Many of them lived in Ghana, and they lived in peace. So when I put all of this into some kind of perspective in my long article, "The Myth of Black Anti-Semitism," major Jewish organizations were outraged and asked for my resignation from Hunter College. Everybody came to my defense, including James Turner. One reason they didn't get my resignation was that the president of Hunter College, who was a woman, told them, "If you can prove him wrong on any point, I will consider asking for his resignation." They could not prove me wrong on any point, and most of my information was taken from books written by Jews.

We do not know people well enough, and we don't know who have been our friends and who have been our enemies. In the meantime, among the number of pamphlets that I've written and circulated was a pamphlet called *Black and White Alliances: A Historical Perspective.* My intention was to show in the pamphlet that we have never had an alliance of consequence with anybody, and that every people, from every ideology, of every religion, that have come among us, have either betrayed us or shown clear indication that they would do so if it were to their benefit. We are an unobligated people. I'm not saying we should not make alliances, but we should make them with the full historical knowledge that no one has done anything for us so outstanding that we need to alter our freedom in order to accommodate them. No one at all. Neither Asians, and least of all the Jews. We're not anti-Jewish, we're pro-Jewish. We remain sentimentally attached to the Jews. We think that the few things they've done for us through philanthropy have made them our friends. If you want to think that, be my guest and go ahead and think it; but if you study their dominance over our community as rent collectors and store owners, you would know that in less than a year they've taken more property out of our community than they've given us in all the years that they've been giving us something. That includes the Rosenwald Fund and every kind of fund, including Annenberg's last gift to the Negro College Fund. Put it all together, it wouldn't equal the amount of money that they take out of our community as real estate owners and as store owners in a six month period.

I had come into the international arena; I was scheduled to attend the International Congress of Africanists in Addis Ababa in 1975. There'd been an argument because Philip Curtin was the American representative who was then on the executive board, and it was time for at least one African American to be on the executive board. We strategized. When I say we, I mean I stayed out of the overt strategizing and let my then lieutenant, James Turner, talk while I sat back and agreed. We had developed a technique with the Africans. We had made contact with the Africans—look when we brothers get together sometimes we can be beautiful. We put a point man in the audience. When he leaned this way that meant yes, if he leaned that way it meant no, and we were voting together—we had our stuff together. We had all the votes we needed before we entered the room. When it was voted that I would be on the executive board, one of the people said, "Who is Professor Clarke, how does he look? Will he stand up so we can at least see?" They didn't even know how I looked. The agreement was that I would serve the African Heritage Studies Association and the African Studies Association, and that I would share information with both groups; and I did. I served until we had the fourth Congress in Zaire. Then Joseph Harris of Howard University became a member of the executive board.

James Turner was at this meeting, doing what politicians are supposed to do—moving around and manipulating, making contacts, feeding me information that I needed. I needed this because I was in these executive meetings, and I couldn't be on the floor all the time. In this service to me, he was more than an able lieutenant; as I think about it now, I should have promoted him to a captain. He was valuable to me because he would move around, listening and talking, while I was attending the executive meetings. It worked out very well. The theme of the meeting was "African Dependency and its Remedy," and the proceedings are in a book that bears that name. It was one of the many books that some people came into my library and liked more often than they thought I did, and took away. This will not happen too often now because I am giving a part of my library, the greater portion, to the Woodruff Library at the Atlanta University Center.

It is essential for an understanding of Pan-Africanism that you understand the nature of dependency. At this closing meeting of the plenary, when I spoke I said, "We have been talking for a week on African dependency and its remedy. There's a book by Cheikh Anta Diop called *Africa: The Politics of A Federated State.* He says more in two paragraphs in his introduction, than we have said in this week long deliberation. In this book, Cheikh Anta Diop points out how the mineral wealth is being stolen out of Africa, how it is being stockpiled in Europe, and what the African will have to do to prepare himself to rescue his wealth for African generations still to come." Most people, including most people teaching about Africa, not only have not read the book, they have not even heard about it. I am now writing a book on Pan-Africanism.

When I was introduced to the work of Cheikh Anta Diop, I spent the next seven years trying to get his work published in English in this country. It took me seven years before the first book came out, *African Origins of Civilization: Myth or Reality.* Then his book, *The Cultural Unity of Africa,* published by the Third World Press, was released. It is a useful work and a fine appraisal of the matrilineal system, not the matriarch concept which is a Hollywood invention. It discusses the role of African female Gods and why African men were secure enough in their society to let the woman's mind go as far as her talent would take it without feeling insecure. I have used this to measure the present day insecurity of Black men who are imitating their European masters who are afraid of women. I've also used it to call attention to what was a stabilizing factor in our life, and one that we once treasured . . . I call it "Big Mamaism." Look at our churches. Behind the scenes, everyone, no exceptions, has a big mama. She's ruling the deacons, and the deacons are ruling the pastors. If you are going to elect a new pastor, it would seem that the men are making a great decision, but every single man has gone home and consulted his big mama on how to cast his vote.

I'm saying that this kind of thing that runs through our life has not made us one mite less men. It has made us more, more of a man, by virtue of the fact that we've realized something that the European man does not realize; that the woman is the giver of life, and that you cannot have a society where one half of that society is barred from full participation in society. You cannot imprison her brain and build a new society because you need the input of all minds. Of course, in the present atmosphere of female lib, the concept of liberation is being misused. Be that as it may, you still have to let her have the ability to let her mind go, and be creative, and to make her creative contribution to the totality of the society without demeaning a single man.

Here's what you need to look at in your African background. Before the first European wore a shoe, or lived in a house that had a window, we already had the female god. Look at Hathor, whose influence spread to India. This is where the whole concept of the sacred cow started. She is sculptured with the torso of a cow, and the head of a female. Look at another great female god, Nut. She was given the assignment of taking down the sun, putting it in her stomach, taking it through her vagina, and hanging it up in the morning. If man trusted woman to symbolically light the world, turn off the sun and turn it back on—we're speaking of symbols now—that means he had no fear of her; and this is why in teaching, I tried to take the students into avenues of information where I have gone.

To give another example, if you understood the Herero war, you would understand that, as glorious as the concept of Namibian independence is, most African states are politically still-born children. Stillborn because they're using a European parliamentary procedure that does not fit Africa. They're trapped with a European economic system that's alien to Africans' economic way of thinking. These are western-educated Africans who've lost too much of their Africanness, including Africa's concept of humanity, and lost a paramount thing essential to Africa's existence—the relationship of the land to nation. If you understand the Malcolm X speech "Message To the Grassroots" you would understand the land basis of nationhood. Land can neither be bought nor sold. A year before the independence of Namibia, international real estate people were buying up land and deciding how much they were going to charge for office space. The Namibians had already agreed not to nationalize their product or nationalize their resources. They have some of the finest diamonds in the world, they have some gold, and they are a fine people. So you've got to understand more than Namibia, you've got to understand the nature of the Herero wars. How can you understand the nature of the Herero wars when people have taught African history without even mentioning the existence of the Herero wars? There are people teaching African history who never read the basic books on Africa.

It's basic that you understand the early anti-colonial writings of George Padmore; if you read his work, *How Britain Rules Africa*, you will find the best description of the Herero wars. You must also read his other book, *Africa: Britain's Third Empire*, as well as his last book, *Pan-Africanism Or Communism?* Then you must also read Caseley Hayford's classic book, *The Truth About the West African Land Quest.* This is what students need, but they will complain, "You are working us too hard." I'd introduce them to literature, to information about our history that they never would have known existed. How did I learn it? By supervising the cleaners at NBC. I had run the typing pool; I took care of the film unit, and later I became head of the cleaners at NBC, and had all that free time during the night shift. Just sitting there, all the jobs had been done, all the offices clean, I had done all the things they paid me for and still had time on my hands. Did I waste it? No. I would sit there and read books. I would check them out of the library in the day and read them at night.

I could use their phones to make phone calls. They couldn't trace the calls. I called Essien Udom in Ibadan. He'd curse me out, and when he'd finish cursing me out, he'd tell me, "I'm glad to hear from you, man. Where the hell are you?" I'd say, "I'm in New York." "How can you pay for a call like this?" I'd say, "I don't have to pay for this call. If I were paying for it, I wouldn't be calling you tonight." I didn't have the slightest idea what time it was in Nigeria, but I made good use of the time. When I had a problem, I could take it up.

About that time CBS discovered that they were giving so few public service programs concerning Black people, that they were about to lose their license. They had to Blacken-up in a hurry. They came to me; they didn't know that I knew they were in trouble. I helped develop a series of Black Studies TV programs. One hundred and eight programs, that ran for six months, half-hour a week. They thought they were going to impress me and took me to dinner at a big club at Columbia University, the Terrace Dining Room. They said to me, "Professor Clarke, we are going to give your lecturers $90.00 per half hour on the air." Suddenly, I had to go to the bathroom. When I came back, I found ten people talking and I said, "I think you are joking. Do you think $90.00 for a public service program, $90.00 for a half hour is impressive?" When I sat down, I said, "I want you to know that I'm going to bring the finest scholars in the African world to this program. Scholars of this caliber wouldn't even walk across the street for $90.00." They offered to pay the lecturers $250.00 for a half an hour on the air. Vincent Harding and Bill Strickland joined me, and we would fashion and put the program together. I would be the coordinator.

The lecturers were leading civil rights activists, including Andy Young, Keith Baird, Richard Moore, Joseph Harris and myself. I did all the background programs and I insisted we begin with the African historical background. I scheduled six programs on the African background. Keith Baird dealt with the

West African background and Africa in general.
Richard Moore dealt with the East African trading
cities. I would then say, "I want a Black producer."
They said, "We don't have a Black producer. We have
an assistant producer who is working on a soap
opera." I said, "Promote him." They promoted him.
We now had a Black producer putting a program on
the air. He was good. He had style. When he said,
"You're on the air," he'd wave his hand down so you
could start talking. I said, "I want to see a Black
hand telling me 'Go ahead, start talking'." I was using
Black power in the true sense and getting results.
Among the lecturers of note were Benjamin Quarles,
St. Clair Drake, Earl Thorpe, and Lerone Bennett. I
still have some of those tapes. The Schomburg
Collection had the video tapes until they lost some of
them, but they still have most of them.

It was a great step forward for me. I let civil
rights activists such as Joanne Grant explain the
Civil Rights Movement. I let them come right into the
studio and made sure they were well paid. I wanted
five programs on Marcus Garvey and Black
Nationalism; I wrote two on Garvey alone, and two on
Black Nationalism. Essien Udom flew all the way
from Nigeria and because he wanted to hide his
money from the Nigerian government—this can be
said . . . it's too late for anybody to do anything about
it—he didn't want the government to take his money
so he wanted to get paid in cash. They didn't know
how to work it out on the books, so I said, "Well,
make the check out to him, let him give it to me, let
me go to the bank and cash the check and give him
the cash." We worked it out that way. Essien Udom
did some excellent lectures. I have the transcript of
every one of those lectures.

In my search for African history, I have had a
second beginning, because this pursuit has been for

me a priesthood. It has been one of the all encom-
passing passions of my existence. It has been a love
affair. For me, it has not been unrequited love. I
have been rewarded. I have established a community of students and scholarly colleagues, and friends
who have come to my assistance and who have
shown love and understanding at a time when I needed it most. If I had to do it again, I would do some
things better; I would choose my friends a little better, I wouldn't let people waste my time, and I would
serve any sincere person who'd come to me. I'd pay
more attention to my health, and I would still have
my eyesight at this age, at this time.

I was a little depressed when I knew that I was
losing my eyesight. I saw no reason for it. I saw
bums who never read a letter, never even wrote home
to mother, with perfect eyesight, walking around the
streets getting on people's nerves. I read more books
than most men see in a lifetime, and I've developed
more understanding from it. My eyes were the great
treasures of my existence. I used them to rescue me
from depression and to enhance my intellectual
being. I could have become thoroughly depressed
about losing my eyesight; however, one night as I was
coming upstairs from my basement office, I heard an
interview on the TV in my living room. Thurgood
Marshall was being interviewed and he was asked,
"Mr. Marshall, what do you think, in the final analy-
sis, needs to be said about you?" He said, "Just tell
them I did the best I could with what I had." I was
impressed with this statement and thought about
myself; a sharecropper's son from the backwoods of
Alabama, growing up in a family that did not read
any book except the Bible. Growing up poor and
hungry; mowing lawns, washing dishes, shining
shoes, airing dogs; coming to New York working in
hotels, all kinds of night jobs and day jobs; studying

at night and working in the day, and sometimes studying in the day and working at night. I was in pursuit of the definition of the role my own people had played in the history of the world; this had been my holy mission, my priesthood. I hope it can be said, whenever the end comes, and I am not hurrying it, because I have no objection to living a thousand years, and I would be useful everyday of that time; however, when it is all over and when I have made every contribution I can make, I hope it can be honestly said of me, "He did the best he could with what he had."

# PART III

———●———

## BLACK STUDIES MOVEMENT

# BLACK STUDIES MOVEMENT

I taught at Cornell when the house (Ujamaa Residential College) was being organized, even when it was talked about being organized. Those were some of the best teaching years of my career. Those were the years after the spin-off from the Civil Rights Movement, when students had a wild confidence in themselves and would research anything. You could hardly tell them that there were certain things they couldn't do because they tried to do everything. They were brilliant students. They're out there in the world going some place today.

What I intend to do is to take Black Studies beyond Blackness, and to look at it as part of an international arena, and to call your attention to the fact that it should have never been called Black Studies in the first place, because it wasn't just about Blackness. Black tells you how you look, but Black does not tell you who you are. The proper name of a people must always relate to land, history and culture, and any time you address any people, if the name you call them fails to relate them to land, history and culture, you have not connected them to their original geography. There's nothing wrong with the word "Black." It's an honorable word, but it's not the name of a people, it's just a color.

You think that this inquiry into the history of African people started with the Civil Rights Movement, the sit-ins and the student protests. No, it started long before that. There is a mistaken assumption that only Blacks have been interested in Black people, or African people; we have not looked at

the broader basis of this study. We have not looked
at European interest in Africa that I call the first fascination. We have not looked at the fact that radical
Black historians were set in motion by what they
learned from radical European historians. There
have been many intellectual trends in Europe. Many
of these trends were going against African trends in
Europe reputing the concept of a people with no history. Unfortunately, of all the books of consequence
created by Blacks, most people read them without
any degree of thoroughness, and some people even
denounce them without having read them at all.
African people have created masterpieces on our history that were not even read by our people.

My focal point right now is to call your attention to the fact that the absence of African people
from the respectful commentary of world history is
not an accidental thing, but a thing that went into a
planning stage. Once the Europeans emerged again
in the fifteenth and the sixteenth centuries they not
only colonized history, they colonized information
about history, then they colonized something else
that they still have colonized. They colonized the
images. Most tragic for us, they colonized the image
of God. Therefore, as I have said before, we are the
only people who worship a God that does not look like
us. People, as a matter of custom, of history, paint
the deity to resemble themselves. Our difficulty is
that you cannot worship a White God over the week-
end, go to that same image the rest of the week and
ask for a job, and fight the same image when you
have to fight Whites. This is the reason too many
times we are willing to fight each other, but not willing to assault a single White policeman. There's no
record of us ever killing a single member of the Ku
Klux Klan, because we are prisoners to image; and
the European not only made you a prisoner to image,

but he made a critical decision in the fifteenth and the sixteenth centuries, and that is, who so ever controls the world it is going to be one of them.

You think that there is an argument between capitalism and communism when Europe is repositioning herself to continue to control the world. Europe's desire to control the world is just as strong on the political left as it is on the right. In that we are a race of dreamers, we quite forget that for us capitalism is a failure, communism is a failure, Western democracy is a fraud, and the European concept of Christianity is a lie. Once you understand that, you stand naked because you've taken off someone else's clothes. Now you have the responsibility of putting on some clothes of your own making, and restoring yourself to a basic rule, that you yourself set in motion before there was a Europe. The history books have reflected that the world waited in darkness for Europe to bring the light, and because the chronology of history places all the greatness within the context of the European emergence, you quite forget that there was no Dark Age in Asia or Africa comparable to the one in Europe. You seem to think there were Dark Ages all over the world. When the Europeans emerged the first time and made contact with African people, there were Europeans writing negatively toward African people; there were also Europeans writing positively toward African people, too.

We have to go back and look at Herodotus and see what Herodotus said. There was an article in the *New York Times* calling some Black historians revisionists. I am one of those they call a revisionist. I'm not a revisionist, I'm a correctionist. I'm not trying to stand history on its head, I'm trying to stand history on its feet. Herodotus, the first of the great eyewitnesses of Africa, said that the tint of complexion of the Ethiopians and the Egyptians was the same.

Because of that, many Whites withdraw their statement that Herodotus is the father of history. I can do
without Herodotus as the father of history. Most
names in his account are wrong anyway! I will say
that Herodotus is one of the first great reporters on
Africa, and he was a good reporter because in his
work—the Rawlinson edition seems to be the best—
he said the Africans told me thus and so, but I tend
not to believe that. Then he said what he did believe.
To approach African history solely from the point of
view of Blackness is dead wrong because many times
Whites have left us some good records we need to
examine.

     We also need to examine Diodorus of Sicily,
Pliny the Elder, Pliny the Son, and Pliny the Younger.
We need to examine Roman historians who wrote
contrary to Roman colonial views of their day and
who left us a good account, because it was from them
that we get an account of the Black Popes; three
Black Popes. I'm not saying that Blacks ruled Rome
when they had three Black Popes, the Romans were
still ruling Rome and ruling the Popes. If you understand what I am saying, you'll understand that presidents don't run this country; there's someone running the president. So they had the Holy See; to hold
the See does not mean you're running the country.
You are just the errand boy of those who are running
the country. You're the front man for those who are
running the country. They had three Black emperors, three African emperors, Septimius Severus being
the most noted of them, and his son Caligula, who
came after him; both were buried in England. One
thing we know much about Septimius Severus is that
he liked the African soul food of that day and could-
n't stand British food. Well, maybe British food is a
little hard to take even now; and he carried his
African cooks with him.

When we come to the Greek period, we come to
Alexander, and we examine Alexander's letters. He
came to Africa at a time when the people from Iran
had overrun both Northern Africa and North East
Africa, and when Africans cried out, "Oh Lord, if you
cannot send me a liberator, send me a conqueror who
will show mercy." This young Greek did not have to
knock at the door very hard; didn't have to fight his
way into Africa; and true to his word, he did show
mercy. He was a rapist. He raided the granary of
Egypt to feed his army. He did what conquerors do,
but he had great respect for the fact that he was at
the home where Greek culture began, and he said so.
He said, "Zeus and Apollo started here!" He wanted
to consult the African Oracles, the great teachers,
and he sent word. He just wanted to ask one question of these great teachers who studied at the great
lodge called Luxor by the Arabs, Thebes by the
Greeks, Waret by the Africans. The teachers asked,
"What is the age of this man?" They said, "Oh, thirty,
thirty-one." The teachers said, "All right. Tell him to
come back in twenty years and maybe he will be
mature enough to ask the kind of questions we might
want to answer." These were great African teachers.

I'm talking about records that Whites have left
us. When you get into your bag and say "I ain't
gonna read this, this is whitey's thing," I want you to
understand the Black radical historians picked up
their cue from White radical historians who were in
rebellion against the European concept. What we are
talking about is not Blackness in itself. What we are
talking about here are the missing pages of the history of the world. This is what we must address ourselves to because a part of humanity is missing from
consideration in world history by their putting our
history outside the history of humanity, the assumption being that we had no history worth considera-

tion. The European learned in the fifteenth and the sixteenth centuries, that you cannot successfully oppress a consciously historical people, because a consciously historical people will not let it happen. So they had to take you out of the commentary of history and program you into dependency to the extent that you think the only way you can make it in the world is to play behind someone else's action and to copy someone else's program. The western-educated African has crippled every state in Africa with this assumption. There is not one state in Africa ruled by Africans that is using an African approach to the rule of government.  They do not understand that the African did not create the nation-state.  The nation-state is a European creation.  The Africans created the territorial state with loose borders, where an entire people, hundreds of thousands, walk across, come and stay for ten years and move on to some other place—people with cattle, people with all kinds of herds.  Africa has size, and nature was kind, so Africans did not have to fight over space; the Europeans developed a temperament that went with their lack of space.

Let's look ten thousand years ago in Europe; the seasons were short between the planting and the harvesting, and the storage life of vegetables was three months at the most.  Everybody had to work, otherwise the ice would come and there wouldn't be enough food for the winter.  If a European man got angry with his mate and said "Get out," she had to cop a plea.  Get out to where?  In all that ice and starve?  Go to the next family?  They had no extra food there to feed her.  Now you see from the very beginning, the temperament of Europe was being shaped by weather, and by circumstances of geography and history.

Now, go to Africa at the same time; they had a

tropical climate. Nature was kind. The forest was
their drugstore. The woman went to the forest and
got something to cure her mate. She domesticated
plants which eliminated his excuse for going on a
hunt too frequently. Once she domesticated plants,
he would more often stay at home. "Maybe we could
do without meat." You will find if you look at archaeology that there were periods, three hundred years at
a time, when the African was a vegetarian. The
woman had furnished enough food for the house,
which meant she eliminated the need for long hunting trips. When the man did go hunting, she cured
the hides for his clothing, the leather for his sandals,
the oils and other things to cure his body, and prepared the meat for him to eat. Now suppose he were
to tell her, "Get out." She'd look at him like he was a
fool. "Get out where? Who gonna feed you? Who
gonna take care of you when you get sick?"

You can now see why an attitude developed in
Africa towards women which was totally different
from the attitude developed towards women in
Europe. You can understand now why the European
male felt more insecure in his relations with women.
There were even cases documented in European
records, where some women displaying religious
peculiarities were labeled as witches and burnt. At
the same time, Africans were developing the first
female God. The African male was having no conflict
about women. The matrilineal system was being
developed, meaning that the lineage comes down
through the female side of the family. It does not
mean matriarchal which is a Hollywood contraption,
for B movies. The female came to power not because
she was a female. She had to wait her turn, but once
it became her turn, nobody could lawfully stop her
unless she declined her turn. Now you can understand why the lack of fear of women allowed for

African female Gods. Hathor, Nut and Maat, are the
three best known of these Gods. The African created
something which he needs to get back, because he
has become too dependent upon European concepts.

Europe tried to defy nature. The African tried
to bring life in harmony with nature. The African created no organized religion. Africans created spirituality which is greater than religion. There are religions with no spirituality that produce preachers like
Jimmy Swaggart, who lacks spirituality, but is a good
performer having seen enough Black Baptist preachers to imitate in order to put on his act.

My main point here is that the lack of fear of
women made a difference in African history. While
Cheikh Anta Diop gives us the best record in his little book *The Cultural Unity Of Black Africa*, you will
find it in many other books—this letting women go as
far as their minds will take them, riding at the head
of their armies, often times all-male armies, and
heading a state. While we get this information mainly from White historians, because there are certain
things that Black historians have not had the time to
do, there are certain things customarily the Africans
assumed that people knew. This is why when
Africans were creating an art excelling that of
Michelangelo, they would not even sign their name on
the painting  because everybody knew who did it.
The people in the village saw him painting it so  he
didn't have to say that's mine; because they knew it
was his. There was no point in signing the name.

Just like a European who went to Africa where
he was doing research of adultery. He kept asking
the Africans questions, "Now, what would happen if
you violated that woman there?" An African said,
"This is simple; I was at the wedding," and walked
away. The European did not understand because
what the African was saying was that since he was at

the wedding he knew she didn't belong to him. I saw her get married to someone else. I know who she belongs to, and I respect that fact. He was saying, "I was at the wedding and I have no confusion about who she belongs to." The Europeans did not understand that.

The first European fascination for Africa, began first with Greek, then Roman historians. When Alexander came into Africa, instead of burning the libraries—and that's one of the greatest myths of history, the burning of the Alexander library—he sent the books home to Aristotle who rewrote a lot of them and put his own name on them; and so a lot of what you think is Aristotle's writing is plagiarism from African writings. That's a topic for another lecture, but if you want to debate it, I would invite you to read George G. M. James's book *Stolen Legacy* and (Yosef) ben-Jochannan's books, *The African Origins of Major Western Religions* and *Africa: Mother of Western Civilization.*

If we were to get these Greek and Roman records, we would find that one of the main reasons why there is an imbalance in record keeping, is that there are certain things the African didn't see fit to write down. This is why you have such a good record of the Hebrew entry into history, because the Hebrews have always been good record keepers; and because they are good record keepers, there came a time when they didn't agree with what they put down, and they became good record changers. The Hebrews entered world history through their visit to Africa. All of our information is taken from their records now, and while they say they were slaves in Africa, except for Biblical mythology there is not one iota of truth or proof that this occurred.

If you read Sir James Fraser's work, *The Folklore of the Old Testament*, it's all there, including the flood stories; or John Jackson's last book of consequence, *Christianity Before Christ.* You think Christianity started with the coming of the Christ, and the Christ figure? It was dogmatized and formalized around his personality, but the concepts existed long before without the name of religion. Where do we get this information? From White records. You go to Alvin Boyd Kuhn's work, *Who Is This King Of Glory?*, in my opinion one of the greatest books written on the Christ story. You will see, what you think are Hebrew texts is a direct steal from African texts. He traces it and documents it. Another book, *Shadow of the Third Century,* tells you what St. Augustine said about the conference at Nicea. He said, "When I read the proceedings, it makes me laugh. These people are trying to give us a religion we had three thousand years ago." We had it under another name. We had an enduring civilization that lasted thousands of years before the first European had a shoe or lived in a house that had a window. When we created a system so enduring, we not only didn't have any jail system, but we had no word in our language that meant jail. There must have been something democratic about it, although you never heard the word until you were taught about Greek democracy and Roman democracy.

When you examine Roman democracy you will find that 85% of the populace were slaves; it was about the same percentage in Greek democracy. So what kind of democracy were they talking about? They were talking about democracy for that elite group that controlled the Senate, while the slaves did their work. This is about the same thing they were talking about in the United States, and you get hung up with the fact that democracy was made for everybody. This country wasn't designed to give democracy to everyone. There's no kidding about it. It was

designed for free White Protestant males, middle-
class and up, those who agreed with the prevailing
political status quo and those who owned property;
and that's who still runs the country. Even while
electing John F. Kennedy as the first Roman Catholic
president in 1960, this country was, and still is, dominated by a Protestant elite.

Look at some of the other historians who gave
us records we need to examine. We need to examine
Godfrey Higgins' work *Anacalypsis*, volumes one and
two, which tell us about the dispersion of African
people throughout the world. We are the most dis-
persed people in all the world, and we are found in
every place in the world—Asia, early Europe. When
the Romans arrived in early England they found
some Black people. What were they doing there? The
Africans entered Central Europe when there was an
unstable climatic period in Africa, a period of high
rainfall and freakish weather, and many Africans
sought space elsewhere. This might explain the
number of Africans in the South Sea Islands. We
know there was a vast migration of Africans to the
Indus Valley; they helped to create the Indus Valley.
There is literature on all of this that we did not create, and we have to look at some of this literature.

We also have to look at the literature concurrent with the rise of Islam. When we go to the literature dealing with the African relationship to Islam
and the African role in the conquest of Spain, once
more we go to European records and Stanley Lane
Poole's book, *The Story of The Moors in Spain*. The
best single chapter on the subject is in John G.
Jackson's work, *Introduction to African Civilization*, in
the chapter called "Africa: The Civilizing Of Europe."
The best work written in recent years on the subject
is by a woman, Eleanor Hoffman—*Land of the
Crescent Moon: Morocco and the Land of the Moors*.

Read her chapter on "The Rape Of Timbuctu;" yes,
"The Rape Of Timbuctu." Very informative, although
somewhat shocking.

We Africans were late in arriving at historical
recording, and we did not place the significance on
historical recording that other people did. While the
literature about the killing of Christians in the
Roman arenas remained available, Cecil B. DeMille
seized on that literature and made big movies out of
it—*Ben Hur* and all those other movies. You quite forgot that there were more African Christians killed in
the amphitheaters of Northern Africa than in the arenas in Rome. No one wrote any literature about this,
and this includes the killing of the African woman,
Hypatia, who started what we now know as the
Sunday School. I get all this from White records. My
message is aimed at the people who assume that if a
White man wrote it, you can't depend on it. Well, fortunately they wrote down a whole lot of things that
we did not write down, and they left us a whole lot of
good records that we did not put together.

In the eighteenth century, European curiosity
about Africa began to grow. Napoleon thought he
would use Egypt as a launching pad for the conquest
of Africa, and he thought he would use Haiti as a
launching pad for the conquest of the Americas. He
was stupid both ways. I know nobody's supposed to
stand at a classy Ivy League school and say Napoleon
was an idiot. But I say that Napoleon was a fascist
and a racist idiot, in spite of the fact that his wife,
Josephine, was partly Black. He brought into Egypt
anthropologists, historians, and archaeologists to tell
him what he wanted to hear, that Egypt was White;
he was going to use this White nation as a launching
pad to conquer those Black people. He made a mistake because one man on the journey was Count
Volney. Count Volney was rich enough not to need

Napoleon's money and not to need Napoleon's favors, so he wrote the contrary view in a book called *Ruins of Empire*. He made a good comparison between the Ethiopians and the Egyptians of that day, because at this time, the Arabs had not completely taken over and parts of North Africa were still populated by Black people.

The great period of European writings on Africa would come in the eighteenth and nineteenth centuries. There were three Germans, among them, Heren. His book, *Herren's Researches*, looks into the economic history of the ancient world. His fourth volume is called *A History of the Commercial Intercourse Between the Egyptians, the Ethiopians and the Carthaginians*. He decries the fact that we have so much information on Carthage but none coming from the Carthaginians. He decries the fact that the history of Carthage is told by adventurers, and conquerors, but not told by the Carthaginians. He speculates on what the victims would have said had the victims written it down.

We could do the same speculation on the indigenous Americans who once populated the West Indies. The destruction of the indigenous Americans made Columbus go to Father Bartolome de Las Casas to get permission to increase the African slave trade in order to save the soul of the Indian. When the Pope sent someone to look into the condition of the Indian, on many islands, there wasn't one Indian left. We know that "Indian" is not their name. Columbus set out for the East Indies, wound up in the West Indies, and slapped an arbitrary name on a people.

When you accept a name that you are not, in time you become what you are not. Richard Moore said, "Slaves and dogs are named by their masters, free men name themselves." So in this country, when we began to accept the word Negro which means nothing, and accept the word colored which means even less, and accept the word Black which only tells you how you look and not who you are, we failed to understand that we had been named, and we must become namers, we must be namers of ourselves.

Moving back to the eighteenth and nineteenth centuries, Herren's work is so well known by scholars of African history, that once they got together among themselves talking shop, if there was a newcomer in the group and they wanted to see whether the newcomer knew enough to be in the group, they would say, "Herren, paragraph one and two, you know, in chapter three" and look at the newcomer. If the newcomer didn't know what they were talking about, he had no business in the group. If you are high class, a high African historian, you are supposed to already know Herren. His research is considered to be the best economic inquiry into the conditions of the ancient world.

The next gentleman on my list was Heinrich Barth. There came a period when some English people decided that honorable trade with the Africans might be more profitable than the slave trade; not all English people, but one group. They were going to send out a team from England to explore and report on the possibilities of honorable trade as against the slave trade. They were a little short on money, so they shopped around for a person who knew some of the languages, who knew botany, who could tell about the plant life and draw some of them, someone hardy enough to travel, who knew basic African cultures and who could write a good account of his travels. They couldn't find that person in England, so they sent to Germany and Blumenblach sent one of his students, Heinrich Barth.

Barth went throughout West and Central Africa. He could speak Arabic so he could take care of that part of it. He could fake a little of the other languages, and besides, some of the people in Africa, being Moslems, could speak Arabic. He would take an Arab-speaking African with him who knew the other African languages. He would dress like an Arab, so he could go in and out of places undetected. He heard of a great body of literature under the name *Tarikh: A History.* He would go to the Imams (preachers) and say "I want to buy some copies of the *Tarikh,*" and they let him know that these sacred histories were not to be sold. Finally, he came to an Imam who said, "I will let you read my copies, and you can copy them." So he stayed there, and read the copies and made a digest history of the kingdoms in inner Africa before the coming of any foreign influence.

Finally, he would write his book *Travels and Discoveries In North and Central Africa.* It is the best single work written on Africa during the middle of the nineteenth century, published in this country in 1857. He would go back to England, but the group that sponsored him was now out of power. They had to keep their promise to publish his findings, so they published a five-hundred copy edition called *A Temple Edition,* in five volumes. I always tell my students if you find the Temple Edition of Heinrich Barth's *Travels and Discoveries in North and Central Africa,* if someone offers it to you for a thousand dollars, pay the thousand dollars and run to me in a hurry because I'm going to give you two thousand and I would have cheated you; it's that valuable. If you look on the rare book market, that particular edition will probably cost you three thousand dollars.

As he entered the city, Barth drew his entry to the city; when he got into the city he would look back and draw it from another angle. He made an excellent, thorough, methodical record of the plant life. He was a disciplined German. Every detail of the scene was captured, he did not leave out anything. You should not dare be without it as a true Africanist scholar. If you say that you're not going to read it because it's written by a White man, you're dead wrong! In the absence of adequate resources and sponsorship, few if any, Blacks could have undertaken that journey had they access to the things that Barth had access to.

The third gentleman was Leo Frobenius. He wrote a five-volume history of African civilization. The English translation was never completed, but was condensed into a two volume work called *The Voice of Africa*. Among the French, Gaston Maspero did a two volume work on African civilization. The first great single work was done by Maurice Delafosse, and condensed into a one-volume work called *The Negroes of Africa*; a horrible title but, that was his title. It's about the history of inner West Africa before the coming of the Europeans.

I'm pointing to literature written by Whites to which we need to pay some attention. There were great states in the Western Sudan. We like to think of Ghana, Mali, and Songhay, but that's a cliche; so much of a cliche that I wish people would stop assuming that these were the only great states in inner West Africa. By doing so you neglect the great Mossi states, the Yoruba states, the Ashanti states, and the Moslem states in the upper Guinea Coast. All this is neglected when you take only the Ghana, Mali, and Songhay approach. In the 1890s, a Frenchman, Felix DuBois, going through all the records, gave us a book called *Timbuctu: The Mysterious*. He went over some work that Black historians still have not gone over because we are so hung-up with ancient Egypt, sometimes the wrong way. We skip from Egypt to transatlantic slavery and forget that there were more than a thousand years of independent states in inner West Africa before slavery. One state, Songhay, existed for 150 years into the slave trade period with its army intact, and they maintained a great university.

When we go to Felix DuBois for his records, not only do we find the record of the destruction of these independent states by the Moroccans, we also learn that there were Africans fighting against Africans: African Moslems against other Africans, North African Moslems against African Moslems in inner Africa. You think that Islam is so purified now, but remember they broke up the last of these states. Also, remember that the Arab slave trade drained Africa of the organization and energy it needed to combat the European slavetraders of the Arab slave trade. This thousand years of Arab slave trade set disorganization in motion. When we want to know exactly how these states were destroyed and the consequences of this destruction, we have to turn to White records. There are no original records written by Blacks. The original records were not available to our scholars because very few of our scholars had facility in the Arab language. Black writers were inspired by records first made by Whites and Africanized Arabs.

My point is that Black Studies goes beyond Blackness. If you are into a Black thing and think that no White person has anything to say, you must understand that many of these White writers that I have referred to have risked their reputations, risked their limbs, risked their very lives to write these books, and they sometimes paid dearly for their publications repudiating the concept that they were dealing with a people who had no history.

We can go to Felix DuBois' work to understand that there was a period in history when there were

only two great universities: The University of Sankore
at Timbuctu, and the University of Salamanca´ in
Spain. The Africans and the Arabs at Salamanca had
preserved the great literature and the great technolo-
gy coming out of what was then the most developed
industrial nation of the late medieval world, China.
China was one hundred and fifty years ahead in maritime skills. The European took this information
about maritime skills and used it to turn on all the
people who had preserved it and subsequently went
into the slave trade that opened up the New World,
showing no gratefulness to the people who had preserved that information. We can go to White records
to get this. Go to a book called *A Vision Of Morocco*
and another called *A Pastoral Democracy*. My point is
that we have to get out of our Black bag, and join the
rest of the human race.

I mean to say that you can be loyal to African
people, while acknowledging that other people have
done some good and preserved some things for you
that are useful. I'm a Pan-Africanist, an African
world Nationalist, and a Socialist. I see no contradiction in being all three simultaneously. My commitment to Africa is not diminished by the fact that I
acknowledge that a lot of the records that helped me
see African history in a broader dimension beyond
Blackness came from White writers. I'm calling upon
you to consider that and broaden the base of what
you're calling Black Studies. I'm also calling upon
you to reconsider the matter and maybe stop calling
it Black Studies, because it's about Africana Studies;
because it is about the African people of the whole
world.

Late in the nineteenth century, the British
were arguing about taking over Nigeria. One of the
early British women journalists, Flora Shaw, went
out to interview the then governor of this region,

before they called it Nigeria. In fact, Nigeria was given its name which she had suggested. It was then under one of the British chartered companies. Eastern Nigeria was called Ibo Land, Western Nigeria was called Yoruba Land, Northern Nigeria was called Hausa Land, and they were ruled separately. She went to Nigeria, fell in love with Lord Lugard, married him, and became Lady Lugard.

She knew Indo-European languages; she also knew some of the African languages, and she decided that she would write a book defending the British right to take over Nigeria. Then she said she's going to do some research for a preface, dealing with what happened in Nigeria and West Africa in general before the coming of the Europeans. What she learned about developments in inner West Africa, and West Africa in general before the coming of the Europeans became so interesting that the material for the preface became the book. The book is called *A Tropical Dependency*. When Nnamdi Azikiwe read the book, he said, "If Africa did it once, Africa will do it again." When Kwame Nkrumah read the book about these great independent states and their leaders, he said, "Well Africa could prove its wealth, its resiliency, and Africa will do it again." This book, written at first to defend colonialism, became the Bible against colonialism. It is the finest work published early in this century and the clearest on Africa before the coming of the Europeans.

Some of the most important of these works that I have been referring to were the first used in an essay that I wrote called "European Interest in Africa: The First Fascination." I want to call your attention to the uses of history in general; and if we're going to use history as an instrument of liberation, we have to pay more attention to what the radical Black writers wrote taking their cues from these radical White writers. Therefore, you have to pay more attention to Chancellor Williams' work, *The Destruction of Black Civilization*, especially his second chapter, "Ethiopia's Oldest Daughter: Egypt," where he traces the origin of Egypt to the South. Lady Lugard does the same thing in her work, *A Tropical Dependency*. James Henry Breasted and other Whites documented the fact that the people who later were called Egyptians came from the South, and the Nile was a great highway bringing people into Africa and out of Africa.

African civilization is the foundation for Western civilization, and one of the reasons why hypocritical Western scholars still feel called on to remove Egypt out of Africa is that they could not attribute to African people an achievement as great as that of the Egyptians. They could not have until Bruce Williams wrote his essay "The Lost Pharaohs of Nubia," detailing the fact that Egyptian civilization started in the South, that pyramid building started in the South, and that Ethiopia and the Sudan are the mothers and fathers of what became Egypt.

They have not read about the "Papyrus of Hunefer" in the *Book Of The Dead*, where the Egyptians said "we came from the head waters of the Nile, near the mountain of the moon where the great god Hapi dwells." Hapi was a god of early Nile Valley spiritual life, which, of course, extended beyond Egypt.

John G. Jackson in his many works, including *Pagan Origins Of The Christ Myth*, traced the Christ stories in several civilizations, each a thousand miles apart. This holds true for his last big book, *Christianity Before Christ*, and his previous book, *Man, God And Civilization*. Man went through many motions before he arrived at what he was willing to accept as a god, and the reason we don't discuss phallic worship is because the mind of Western man can't deal with the fact that there was a time when man thought his penis was a thing of holiness and went into court and swore on it. He did this with great care because if he was proven a liar, there were two men with a stone to crush it. So he had to think twice. This is where the phrase "to testify" came from. If you loved a woman well enough, you would testify in her behalf, which is supreme love indeed.

The mind of some people is a little evil where sex is concerned, and I won't dwell on it too much myself at this juncture. Having other things to do, we do not see fit to trace man in search of a god: sun worship, phallic worship, and nature worship. John G. Jackson in his book, *Man, God and Civilization,* has done most of this work, and his last work, *The Ages Of Gold And Silver,* he said, is his crowning achievement. The scholarship of earlier White historians helped to bring into being men like J. C. deGraft Johnson whose work *African Glory* was the first African history written by an African. All of this would lead to Africa's greatest single historian produced in our time, Cheikh Anta Diop, and his last work, *Civilization or Barbarism.* In this book, he takes off his gloves, and with no more hinting, says this is it. The Black historians, like William Leo Hansberry, whose books were published posthumously (*Ethiopian Notebook* and *Africa Seen By The Greeks*), were set in motion by non-Black historians.

General Massey needs special mention because he was an Englishman who said that Christianity was stolen from the Africans. He wrote a six-volume work, and spent almost forty years in writing it: *Egypt: Light of the World,* two volumes; *Natural Genesis,* two volumes; and *Book of the Beginning,* two volumes. If there was any doubt about who the Egyptians were, that doubt is put to rest in the works of Gerald Massey. His greatest

American disciple was Alvin Boyd Kuhn, whose best-known works are *Shadow of the Third Century* and *Who Is This King of Glory?* His book, *The Rebirth of Christianity*, and another work published posthumously, *The Canons of Knowledge*, are well worth looking at.

My final point, in looking at this situation from both the Black side and the White side, is to call to the attention of Black students that we have survived the longest and the most brutal holocaust in human history. While the one in Europe was wrong—it was wrong if they killed six million, it was wrong if they killed only six, it was wrong period—it was in essence a matter started in Europe by Europeans and should have been resolved in Europe by Europeans. European racism that had spent itself outside of Europe, turned inward on itself within Europe. It was an internal matter of the Europeans. Now, for the slave trade that the Arabs engaged in, if you want to name a people who have a case against the Arabs, we're the ones that have a case.

Having survived this denial of our basic humanity as a people, having been systematically read out of history, if all we have done is just to survive, given the pressure, our survival alone would have removed from us forever the stigma of inferiority; because no inferior people could have survived such torture for so many long years. I think faith has spared us for a mission in history, not to oppress any people, but to participate in a campaign to end oppression of all people. Not necessarily to forgive or forget what has happened, but to let people who committed crimes against us know that we'll be ready to deal with them in an entirely different way if they repeat the crime. We are the most fortunate of the people on this earth, because we have a mission that is worthy of world respect; we must stop all the nonsense about divisions between African people. We must remember that the slave ship to this hemisphere brought only African people.

There was an argument in my class between Caribbean people and African people and African Americans. The classroom is overlooking Lexington Avenue in New York City. I said, one by one, I want all of you to go down to Lexington Avenue and count the number of cabs that pass before one picks you up. An average of twenty-one cabs passed before anyone picked up the African, the Caribbean person, or the African American. I pointed out the obvious to students: You might have passed my academic test but you failed the taxi cab test. That bigoted White cab driver is a better pan-Africanist than you are; he sees all of you as one people. He doesn't care who's from the West Indies, who's from Africa, who's from Georgia; he don't want to ride with any of you.

I told a White female student, you go down and count the number of cabs that pass before they pick you up. She was almost to the sidewalk and her hand was almost up, and three cabs stopped. I said, she is a citizen and the rest of you are subjects. Don't get confused between the two. No one brought you here to give you democracy. In a nation of immigrants, you are the immigrants whose ancestors came against their will. They were the only immigrants who came with an invitation. The nature of the invitation will not be discussed here, but there were plenty of jobs for us, no unemployment, and no pay either. Our three hundred years of labor laid the economic foundation for this nation. Five hundred years of exploiting Africa, one way or the other, laid the basis for the modern technical, scientific world.

We participated in the changing of the world; the world would never be the same after the fifteenth and the sixteenth centuries, and our exploitation did

it.   Other people were hit less than we, and they
became extinct.   I think faith has saved us for a purpose and a mission, and I think that mission is to
unify all African people throughout the world through
a single pan-African program to reclaim every inch of
Africa for African people, all twelve million square
miles of it.   To restore African dignity to Africa, to stop
imitating Europe, to put Africa back on the road to
believing in itself again, producing for itself, and to
end this whole cultism around consumerism and
begin to produce the things we eat, the clothes we
wear, and the transportation we use.   We need to
restore self-reliance, because it is a terrible thing for
a people to be out of power; and when a people are
out of power for so long, they long desperately for
power and when they get close to it they panic,
because they have not rehearsed for power.   One of
my professors told me years ago, "John, we will have
no problem getting to the door of the Promised Land,
but we will get to the door of the Promised Land and
we will bunch up and start an argument as to
whether we cross the threshold with our left foot or
our right."

      That's where we are today, arguing at the door
of the Promised Land, following people who don't
know where they are going.   Following people who
think they are socialists and forgetting that our
socialism, that we had before Europeans had shoes,
became socialism in Europe.   Our communalism,
that we had before Europeans had houses with win-
dows, became communism in Europe.   If we want a
new way of life, and if we want communism or capitalism, we don't have to go to Europe for it, we can go
within ourselves.   We have to establish and reestab-
lish a system of self-belief.   We will not come to power
to establish a Black branch of the Ku Klux Klan, we
are too smart to use our energy that way; this would

be a useless dissipation of energy. If faith or God or whatsoever has spared us, it has spared us to help restore humanity to ourselves and to all mankind and to teach a lesson that will not only be good for our children, but for children still unborn.

We should never have gotten into this campaign against apartheid because apartheid is not the real issue anyway. The real issue in South Africa is European control of the mineral wealth of the world. They can destroy apartheid tomorrow, and the Africans would still have a problem. The Africans living outside of Africa have the technical knowledge to contribute in partnership with Africans in the homeland to the transformation of Africa to make it produce for its own self and to build universities in Africa for African people.

George Lenon once said, "We need a generation of Africans educated in Africa by other Africans, for the express purpose of training Africans to serve Africa who will not give a damn who likes what they're doing or not." We have spent too much time seeking our oppressor's approval. We have to stop caring about his approval because he will not approve of anything that will make us free of his domination, because he is intent on dominating the world.

My point is that if we reclaim all of Africa, all of those islands in the Caribbean, the islands of the Pacific populated by people of African descent, united with the millions of Africans in India, we will go into the twenty-first century with a billion people, a billion African people, and we will be the second, if not the first largest ethnic group on the face on the earth. You don't have to debate about who will be your ally, if you are an ally to yourself. Chances are you may need an ally. You must believe in yourself because no one, east or west, has made any space for you, and we have to start with our history in this restoration.

We must start by acknowledging the fact that we might have to step back in order to step forward. We might have to go back to what I call the fork in the road where we misread the sign boards, and once we read the sign boards correctly, and find the arrow pointing toward unity, self-reliance, and Pan-Africanism, this might be the road that leads us home. Travelling down that road, we must restore our humanity first; we will be changing the world by changing ourselves first. This might be our holy mission. It might be the legacy that we can leave for our children, and their children still unborn.

# BIBLIOGRAPHY

Barth, H. (1965). *Travels and Discoveries in North & Central Africa.* Vol. 1-5, London: Frank Cass & Co., Ltd.

ben-Jochannan, Y. A. A. *African Origins of Major Western Religions.* New York: Alkebu-lan Books.

—. *Africa: Mother of Western Civilization.* New York: Alkebu-lan Books.

Bennett, L. Jr. (1975). *The Shaping of Black America.* Chicago: Johnson Publishing Co., Inc.

Breasted, J. H. (1967). *A History of Egypt.* New York: Bantam Matrix Books.

Danquah, J. B. (1958). *The Akan Doctrine of God.* London: Frank Cass &Co., Ltd.

—. (1958). *Obligation to Akan Society.* London: Frank Cass & Co., Ltd.

deGraft-Johnson, J.C. (1969). *African Glory...The Story of Vanished Negro Civilizations.* New York: Walker & Co.

Delafosse, M. (1969). *The Negroes of Africa.* New York: Negro University Press.

Diop, C. A. (1959). *Cultural Unity of Africa.* Chicago: Third World Press.

—. (1960). "Black Africa: The Economic & Cultural Basis of a Federated State." Paris: *Presence Africaine Magazine.*

—. (1974). *African Origins of Civilization: Myth or Reality.* Westport, CN.: Lawrence Hill & Co.

—. (1991). *Civilization or Barbarism.* Westport., CN: Lawrence Hill & Co.

DuBois, F. (1969). *Timbuctoo the Mysterious.* New York: Negro University Press.

Fraser, J. (1919). *Folklore of the Old Testament.* 3 Vols., London: MacMillan & Co.

Frobenius, L. (1913). *The Voice of Africa.* London: Hutchinson & Co.

Hansberry, W. L. (1981). *African History Notebook.* Washington, D.C.: Howard University Press.

—. (1981). *Africa & Africans As Seen by Classical Writers.* Washington, D.C.: Howard University Press.

Herren, A. H. L. *Historical Researches into the Politics, Intercourse & Trade of the Principal Nations of Antiquity.* London: Henry G. Bohn, MDCCCXLVI.

Higgins, G. (1965). *Anacalypsis.* Vol. I&II, New York: University Books, New Hyde Park.

Hoffman, E. (1965). *Land of the Crescent Moon: Morocco & the Land of the Moors.* New York: Chilton Books.

Jackson, J. G. (1933). *Was Jesus Christ A Negro?* New York: The Author's Publication.

—. (1938). *Christianity Before Christ.* New York: The Blyden Society.

—. (1937). *The African Origins of the Legend of the Garden of Eden.* New York: The Author's Publication.

—. (1990). *Ages of Gold and Silver.* Austin: TX: American Atheist Press.

Jackson, J. G and W. N., Huggins. (1970). *Introduction to African Civilization.* New York: University Books, New Hyde Park, reprinted.

—. (1934). *A Guide to the Study of African History.* New York: Federation of History Clubs.

James, G. G. M. (1954). *Stolen Legacy.* New York: Philosophical Library.

Kuhn, A. B. (1944). *Who is the King of Glory?.* Elizabeth, NJ: Academy Press.

—. (1949). *Shadow of the Third Century, A Reevaluation of Christianity.* Elizabeth, NJ: Academy Press.

Lane-Poole, S. (1986). *The Story of the Moors in Spain.* London: G. Putnam & Son.

Lugard, F. S. (1905). *A Tropical Dependency.* London: J. Nisbet & Co.

Massey, G. (1970). *Egypt: Light of the World.* 2

Vols. New York: Samuel Weiser, Inc.

—. (1974). *Natural Genesis.* 2 Vols. New York: Samuel Weiser, Inc.

—. (1881). *Book of Beginnings.* 2 Vols. London: Williams & Norgate.

Padmore, G. (1936). *How Britain Rules Africa.* London: Wishart Books, Ltd.

—. *Africa: Britain's Third Empire.* Dobson, D., Ltd., *Pan-Africanism or Communism.* New York: Doubleday/Anchor Books.

Powell, R. (1937). *The Human Side of A People and the Right Name.* New York: The Philemon Co.

(1966). *Tarikh.* Vol 1., No. 3. New York: Humanities Press.

Volney, C. (1921). *The Ruins or a Survey of the Revolution of Empires.* London: Pioneer Press.

Williams, B. (Sept.–Oct. 1980). "The Lost Pharaohs of Nubia." *Archaeology Magazine.*

Williams, C. (1974). *Destruction of Black Civilization: Great Issues of Race from 4500 B.C.–2000 A.D.* Chicago: Third World Press.

# ABOUT THE AUTHOR

To begin observance of its twentieth anniversary in March, 1990, the Africana Center invited John Henrik Clarke to begin its celebration with this series of distinguished lectures.

John Henrik Clarke was born on January 1, 1915 in Union Springs, Alabama, the son of John and Willalla (Mays) Clarke. He attended elementary and secondary school in Columbus, Georgia and college in New York City (New York University and the New School for Social Research) and in Africa (University of Ibadan in Nigeria and the University of Ghana in Accra). In 1970, he received an honorary Doctor of Humane Letters degree from the University of Denver.

A prolific writer and popular lecturer, he developed and coordinated the CBS television series, "Black Heritage: The History of Afro-Americans." He has published poetry, short stories, and historical studies. The author and editor of more than two dozen books, he was founding chairman of the Black and Puerto Rican Studies Department at Hunter College of the City University of New York and founding President of the African Heritage Studies Association. He was associate editor of *Harlem Quarterly* and *Freedomways* and editor of *African Heritage*.

In 1986, when he retired as the first Thomas C. Hunter Professor at Hunter College, the Africana Studies and Research Center named its 12,000 volume facility, the John Henrik Clarke Library in recognition of his pioneering work in the field of Africana Studies, his invaluable contribution to the development of the curriculum at the Africana Center, and his support of its faculty, staff, and students.

John Henrik Clarke is most noted for reminding us that "History is not everything, but it is a starting point. History is a clock that people use to tell their time of day. It is a compass they use to find themselves on the map of human geography. It tells them where they are, but more importantly, what they must be."